THE VITAL TRIANGLE

The Vital Triangle

China, the United States, and the Middle East

JON B. ALTERMAN AND JOHN W. GARVER

THE CSIS PRESS

**Center for Strategic
and International Studies**
Washington, D.C.

Significant Issues Series, Volume 30, Number 2
© 2008 by Center for Strategic and International Studies
Washington, D.C.
Printed on recycled paper in the United States of America
Cover design by Robert L. Wiser, Silver Spring, Md.
Cover photograph: Visiting Saudi king Abdullah walks beside Chinese president Hu
Jintao during a review of the honor guard welcoming ceremony at the Great Hall
of the People in Beijing, January 23, 2006.
© Frederic J. Brown/AFP/Getty Images

11 10   5 4

ISSN 0736-7136
ISBN 978-0-89206-529-5

Library of Congress Cataloging-in-publication Data
Alterman, Jon B., 1964–
   The vital triangle : China, the United States, and the Middle East / Jon B. Alterman
and John W. Garver.
        p. cm. — (Significant issues series)
   ISBN 978-0-89206-529-5 (pbk. : alk. paper)
   1. United States—Foreign relations—China. 2. China—Foreign relations—United
States. 3. United States—Foreign relations—Middle East. 4. Middle East—Foreign
relations—United States. 5. China—Foreign relations—Middle East. 6. Middle
East—Foreign relations—China. I. Garver, John W. II. Title. III. Series.
   JZ1480.A57C595 2008
   327.73051—dc22   2008014089

CONTENTS

ACKNOWLEDGMENTS

Many people around the globe helped turn this idea into a published product. In Beijing, Professor Wang Suo Lao of Beijing University was a consistently helpful and supportive colleague, and our hosts at the major research institutions in the city added greatly to our appreciation of Chinese perspectives. In the Middle East, the Emirates Center for Strategic Studies and Research (ECSSR), under the leadership of Dr. Jamal al-Suweidi, generously cosponsored a successful conference that brought together researchers from the Arab world, the United States, and China. Nicolas Heard of the ECSSR did yeoman duty pulling together all of the various strands to make the conference go smoothly. Back in the United States, Justin Leites added considerable elegance to some of the language, and U.S. Navy fellow Dan Murphy of CSIS was a thoughtful and valuable colleague. The staff and interns of the CSIS Middle East Program provided crucial research and administrative support. In particular, John Chen was an exemplary researcher during a summer internship, and Deputy Director Haim Malka and Program Coordinator Greg Brosman helped ensure that things stayed on track both intellectually and administratively.

CHAPTER ONE

INTRODUCTION

Chinese premier Hu Jintao's visit to Washington in the spring of 2006 seemed star-crossed. A Falun Gong protestor heckled him for several minutes on the White House lawn and had to be removed, and a White House announcer mixed up China's formal sovereign name with the name preferred by the nationalist government on Taiwan. At one point, confusion about staging caused President Bush to usher Premier Hu off the podium, only to yank him back when the mistake was discovered.[1] Throughout the four-day visit, neither the American hosts nor Chinese guests seemed wholly comfortable. Instead, each seemed preoccupied as it sought to maneuver between the sensibilities of politics at home along with the sensitivities of the other great power.

From Washington, Hu went on to Riyadh, Saudi Arabia, where the mood was much different. A carefully scripted tour went off without a hitch, and the two countries signed agreements strengthening cooperation in several areas, including energy exploration and security. Hu also became one of the first foreign leaders ever to address Saudi Arabia's Consultative Council, the country's appointed parliamentary body.[2] There were no protestors, no uncomfortable conversations, and no damage control. Two nations made narrow agreements in their mutual interest, uncomplicated by either country's sense of its global role or its global responsibility. Saudi Arabia has gas and oil; China needs gas and oil. On that basis, agreements were made.

Hu's Arabian sojourn piqued interest in the United States, in part because the U.S. agenda with each country is so complicated. The U.S.-Saudi relationship has been close for more than a half century,

1

but what began as a relationship in the 1930s principally about oil and energy security has evolved into one that also concentrates heavily on counterterrorism, radicalization, the Arab-Israeli conflict, Iraq, Iran, and human rights. Traditionally, each country's ambassador to the other deals directly with the executive of the other state rather than working through Foreign Ministry counterparts. The intimacy of that relationship during the Cold War was clear not only through Saudi support for *mujahideen* fighting the Soviet Union in Afghanistan, but through a whole series of other shared efforts, both overt and covert, to serve mutual strategic interests.[3]

The events of September 11, 2001, shook the Saudi-U.S. relationship, but they did not recast it. Government-to-government cooperation across a wide number of fields today is deep and broadening, even as the Saudi and U.S. publics continue to eye each other warily. The bilateral governmental relationship has become so laden with importance that one White House official privately remarked in 2006, "Everything that matters to us in the Middle East goes through Riyadh."[4]

The Sino-American relationship is, in many ways, an older one, dating back to nineteenth century missionaries and traders. Yet, the Communist revolution set China and the United States as adversaries for decades, and it has only been for the last 35 years, since 1971, that common interests regarding the Soviet Union began to foster cooperative relations between the United States and the People's Republic of China (PRC). The relationship broadened greatly in 1978 when Deng Xiaopeng began to lead China toward economic engagement with the world. Still, many in both countries see the others not as partners or global actors with shared interests, but as competitors in both economic and military spheres. Americans fear that China seeks to displace U.S. primacy, while Chinese fear that the United States seeks to contain China in the Pacific. Further, some in the United States see China as an abuser of human rights that coddles oppressive regimes such as Iran and Sudan and enables them to escape the strictures of U.S.-led sanctions. They see China not so much as a fellow great power, but a rising superpower that aims to undermine U.S. hegemony. Finally, a growing number of Americans are beginning to fear the impact of Chinese trade with and investments in the United States. They fear Chinese holdings of U.S. debt, the potential sale of U.S. assets to China's new sovereign wealth fund, and the sale of companies in sensitive technology industries to a potential military competitor. In China there are similar deep apprehensions about U.S. policies.

It is not, then, that the United States is hostile toward either the Middle Eastern states or China; it has deep and complicated relations with each. Those relations are robust and strategic, and they cover a wide range of activities. But just as those relations encompass a wide range of shared interests, they also encompass serious concerns with strong constituencies in the United States. Protest accompanies most leaders of both China and Middle Eastern states when they visit the United States, and critical words pour out on the floors of Congress.

Similarly, anti-Americanism has spread its roots in both the Middle East and in China. In the Middle East, there is widespread resentment toward the United States over a variety of issues. Some are narrower and policy related, such as the U.S. approach to the Arab-Israeli conflict and U.S. actions in Iraq. Others are more general, from seeing the United States as the principal guarantor of security to authoritarian regimes, to fearing the United States as a rapacious, homogenizing cultural juggernaut that threatens to obliterate local norms and customs. In the eyes of many Arabs, the United States is a superpower that needs a comeuppance, and one that could use a competitor to balance its reckless ways.[5]

In China, the accepted foreign policy orthodoxy is that the United States is a hegemonic power that aggressively pursues its own interests at others' expense. Many analysts see recent U.S. efforts to reform the Middle East and replace unpalatable rulers as undermining stability rather than supporting it. In this way, they see the United States acting against the interests not only of China, but of the international community more broadly.[6]

By contrast, Chinese–Middle Eastern relations are far simpler and, some would say, shallow. Gone are the days when China sought to be the reliable friend of liberation movements around the world and thus the foe of most established governments. Now, a thirst for energy guides much of China's policy in the Middle East, with other commercial, military, and diplomatic interests playing a subsidiary role. Because Middle Eastern governments control much of what China seeks in the Middle East, China has sought to broaden its relationships with these governments.

These governments, in turn, have been tremendously impressed with the way in which China's economy has grown under a durable authoritarian system. They have also been gratified that the Chinese have made no appeals to upend their domestic practices and that China puts its millions into promoting trade rather than working to strengthen civil society groups that seek the strength to push for internal reforms. China is no longer the foe of regimes in the Middle East, but their friend; the country has gone from being a revolutionary power to being a status quo power. The United States in some regards has undergone a transformation in the opposite direction as regards the Middle East.

On the popular level, China carries little of the baggage that the United States does in the Middle East. Local publics (and their governments) conveniently elide China's rigorous atheism and its ongoing battle with Muslim Uighur separatists in the Western provinces, and they see a country that manufactures affordable goods and communicates respect. The Chinese public seems to see the Middle East as a place wracked by conflict, one that is strategically important, but that poses no challenge to China. Chinese officials seek to develop a kind of "positive multipolarity" that enables China to be the friend of all and the enemy of none. The task is made easier by the fact that China's relationship with the Middle East is one of calculation rather than emotion; for Western powers, there is often quite a bit of both.

This volume explores the complex interrelationships between China, the Middle East, and the United States—what we call the "Vital Triangle." There is surely much to be gained from continuing what we would see as two-dimensional work—China and the United States, the United States and the Middle East, and China and the Middle East. Such scholarship has a long history, and it no doubt has a long future. But it is the three-dimensional equation—which seeks to understand the effects of the Chinese–Middle Eastern relationships on the United States, the U.S.–Middle Eastern relationships on China, and the Sino-American relationship on the Middle East—that draws our attention. It is this approach that captures the true dynamics of change in world affairs and the spiraling up and spiraling down of national interests. Central to our understanding is a belief that if any one of the three sides of this triangular relationship is unhappy, it has the power to make the other two unhappy as well. The stakes and the intimacy of the interrelationship highlight not only the importance of reaching accommodation, but also the potential payoff of agreement on common purpose.

∾

THE BINDING CORD IN THE TRIANGULAR RELATIONSHIPS between China, the Middle East, and the United States is energy. Energy led the United States to the Middle East in the 1930s, it leads China to the region today, and over the last 75 years, it has led the Gulf from abject poverty to prosperity. The United States consumes approximately 25 percent of the world's oil production; China in 2005 consumed about 7 percent of global oil production, though that was projected to double to 14 percent by 2015. China's booming economy accounted for approximately 50 percent of the annual growth in world oil consumption in 2006 and 43 percent of that growth in 2007.[7] Although conservation efforts are afoot in both countries, each will remain highly reliant on petroleum products to support their economies long into the future.

In the global hunt for oil, the United States had a huge head start. The U.S. government has been intimately involved in developing the oil industry in the Middle East since the 1930s, as U.S. companies (and their British counterparts) carried out the initial prospecting in the barren lands of the Arabian Peninsula. Beginning in 1933, a consortium of U.S. oil companies (starting with Standard Oil of California, which became Chevron, and coming to include the precursors to Exxon, Texaco, and others) established the Arabian-American Oil Company, or Aramco. The company was a joint Saudi-American venture until the Saudi side acquired a 100 percent stake in the company in the 1980s. In its almost half century of binational ownership, Aramco created a park-like campus in Dhahran that not only made Americans feel at home, but also made Saudi managers feel like they were in the United States. As Saudis came to play increasingly large roles in management, they did so largely on American terms. National oil companies arose throughout the Middle East in the 1950s and 1960s, and local states took over their operations, yet these companies in many ways remained American operations, even when they ceased to be U.S.-owned. The structure was American, the working language was English, and, most important, the ethos of the institution resonated with U.S. values.

For many decades, the Western orientation made immense sense, because the major consuming countries were Western as well. Even growth in Japanese and Korean consumption proceeded smoothly under a Western model, so great were the impacts of the U.S. postwar occupations on each country. When China became a net importer of oil in 1993, and when its Middle Eastern imports quickly skyrocketed, the existing business model seemed less adequate. China had its own needs, its own interests, and its own ways of doing things, and they did not always fit with the commercial model that had emerged under Western tutelage.

As China's oil imports grew in the 1990s, Chinese national companies have sought equity shares in oil projects, hoping that such stakes will be less subject to interruption than oil purchased on the open market. China has a unique approach to the international energy marketplace, in that the government "simultaneously strives to retain control of the industry while encouraging its state oil companies to be aggressively entrepreneurial."[8] China has three major oil and gas companies—the Chinese National Petrochemical Corporation (Sinopec), the China National Offshore Oil Company (CNOOC), and the China National Petroleum Corporation (CNPC). In 2000, CNPC established a subsidiary, PetroChina, which is partly financed by private equity with a clear profit orientation. Sinopec alone is engaged in some 120 oil and gas projects in the Middle East, and currently approximately 10 percent of China's oil imports globally come from fields in which China's state-owned oil companies have an equity stake.[9] But as China looks around the world for oil equity holdings, it finds that most of the proven reserves of oil are already spoken for, much of it by the national oil companies of producer nations that control 85 percent of the world's traded oil.[10]

About half of China's imported oil, and about 20 percent of China's total oil supply, now comes from the Middle East. In 2005 about 40 percent of China's oil supply was imported. Over the past decade China has tried to diversify its oil imports to include less volatile sources, and these efforts have paid off in increased imports, including from the states of the former Soviet Union and Latin America. Sub-Saharan Africa is China's most promising new supplier, having increased its share of total imports from 1.8 percent in 1992 to about 28 percent in 2005. Yet as figure 1.1 shows, China's demand for imported oil is growing so rapidly, and Middle Eastern petroleum resources are simply so much richer than those of other regions, that the percentage of China's imported oil coming from the Middle East hardly changed from 1990 (47.8 percent) to 2005 (49.7 percent).

In the United States, by contrast, 27.4 percent of imported oil came from the Middle East in 2007, with Canada and Mexico combining to outweigh the Middle East share.[11] The ratio of proven reserves to production in various oil-producing regions suggests that the Middle East will continue to be the dominant source of Chinese oil imports. According to one report, 70 percent of China's imported oil will be coming from the Middle East by the end of 2015.[12]

In recent years, other issues in the Middle East have fueled tension between the United States and China. In 2004, U.S. secretary of state Colin Powell referred to events in Darfur as "genocide" and called for

Figure 1.1. China's Oil Imports by Region of the World

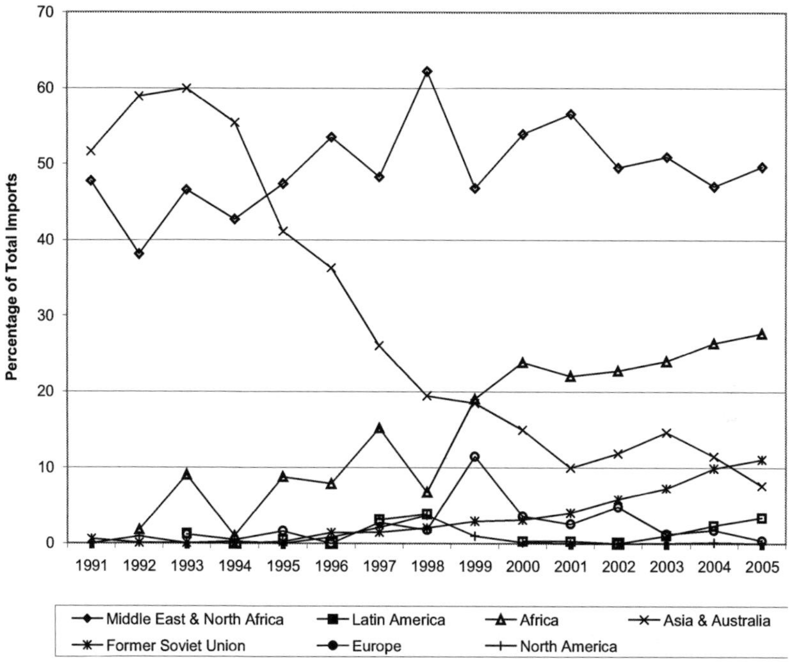

Source: *Zhongguo haiguan tongji nianjian* [China customs statistical yearbook] (Beijing: Chinese Customs Statistical Bureau, various years).

concerted international action to force change on the government in Khartoum, to the apparent frustration of China's permanent representative to the United Nations.[13] China has been a reluctant partner on U.S. efforts to tighten international sanctions on Iran as a consequence of its nuclear program, and a new raft of U.S.-imposed secondary sanctions on countries and businesses investing in Iran could have direct implications for Chinese investment there. Further, any hint of Chinese assistance to the Iranian armed forces—even dual-use materials—could be highly inflammatory to a U.S. public that is watching American soldiers fighting forces in Iraq that are at least partly backed by Iran and view with concern the prospect of an Iranian-U.S. military confrontation in the Gulf.

China's rising concentration on the Middle East as an energy resource, and the enduring U.S. concentration on the region as a key strategic battleground, creates the possibility of competition or even military conflict that could spill over to other regions of the world. In addition, and perhaps even more troubling to Chinese security professionals, Sino-American tensions elsewhere in the world could lead to Sino-American conflict in the Middle East. Such an eventuality could cut China off from access to energy, since the United States controls the sea lanes on which oil to China travels. Although China and the United States have thus far not clashed in the Middle East, the consequences of such conflict are serious enough that they bear prolonged examination.

It is that prospect that drove this study, the culmination of a two-year effort to examine not only the sources of potential conflict between China, the United States, and the Middle East, but also steps that might be taken to prevent such a conflict from breaking out. The study took the coauthors to both China and the Middle East for in-depth discussions with policymakers and scholars. A week of sustained interviews in Beijing in the spring of 2007 and a conference bringing together U.S., Chinese, and Arab experts in Abu Dhabi in the autumn of 2007 punctuated the exchange of ideas.

This study begins with an exploration of the Chinese perspectives on the China–Middle East–U.S. triangle, followed by the Middle East, and then those of the United States. A final concluding section points forward and offers a set of policy recommendations.

To a degree, it is the finding of this study that China is not and does not seek to be a rival of the United States in the Middle East. Indeed, China's diplomacy is very clearly oriented toward not confronting the United States in the Middle East (or elsewhere, in most cases). In addition, China has benefited tremendously from the security protection that the United States extends for Chinese interests.

At the same time, however, many Chinese believe that U.S. actions in the region have undermined stability and thus hurt Chinese interests. There is an ongoing temptation for China to deal directly with states that the United States is seeking to isolate, thereby picking up valuable assets at fire sale prices. In other words, although there is no immediate conflict, the conditions under which conflict might arise are not hard to imagine.

Overwhelmingly, however, the United States, China, and the governments of the Middle East share a deep interest in regional stability and the free flow of energy, and we believe that those common interests create a platform for cooperation that can enhance not only security in the Middle East, but also Sino-American relations more generally. The

Middle Eastern piece of this puzzle is a small but significant one, and we are grateful for the opportunity to help sketch out its dimensions.

Notes

1. Joseph Kahn, "In Hu's Visit to the U.S., Small Gaffes May Overshadow Small Gains," *New York Times,* April 22, 2006, http://www.nytimes.com/2006/04/22/world/asia/22china.html.

2. Hassan Fattah, "Hu's Saudi Visit Signals a Change in the Gulf," *International Herald Tribune,* April 24, 2006, http://www.iht.com/articles/2006/04/23/news/hu.php.

3. For example, Saudi Arabia contributed to U.S. efforts to support the Nicaraguan Contras in the 1980s, and the United States supplied advanced warning systems to Saudi Arabia at the same time and continues to train the Saudi National Guard.

4. Senior White House official's conversation with Jon Alterman, October 12, 2006.

5. Amre M. Moussa, "A Nationalist Vision for Egypt" (interview), *Middle East Quarterly* (September 1996), http://www.meforum.org/article/315.

6. Authors' interviews in China, May 2005 and March 2007.

7. Energy Information Administration, "Short-Term Energy Outlook," February 2008, www.eia.doe.gov/emeu/steo/pub/xls/Fig5.xls.

8. Henry Lee and Dan A. Shalmon, "Searching for Oil: China's Oil Initiatives in the Middle East," Environment and National Resources Program, Belfer Center for Science and International Affairs, John F. Kennedy School of Government, Harvard University, January 2007, 3, http://belfercenter.ksg.harvard.edu/files/china%20oil%20h%20lee%202007.pdf.

9. Anthony Skinner, "Fueling the People's Republic," *The Middle East* (January 2008), 40.

10. Lee and Shalmon, "Searching for Oil," 8.

11. U.S. Energy Information Administration, "International Petroleum (Oil) Imports and Exports," http://www.eia.doe.gov/emeu/international/oiltrade.html#USTrade.

12. Frederick Stakelbeck, "China Looks to the Middle East," *Alexander's Gas and Oil Connection,* September 27, 2006.

13. Glenn Kessler and Colum Lynch, "U.S. Calls Killings in the Sudan Genocide," *Washington Post,* September 10, 2004, http://www.washingtonpost.com/wp-dyn/articles/A8364-2004Sep9.html.

CHAPTER TWO

CHINA

CHINA'S MANAGEMENT OF CONFLICTING INTERESTS

Beijing's policies in the Middle East are an attempt to balance two sets of competing interests. On the one hand, Beijing seeks to expand Chinese cooperation with each country in the region. Middle East oil and trade support China's continued economic development. Growing diplomatic influence in the region supports China's "rise" to high international status and helps provide a hedge against Western and especially U.S. insistence on global political norms.

At the same time, Beijing does not want its emerging role in the Middle East to antagonize the United States. Beijing regards good Sino-American relations as essential for China's continued overall economic development. Moreover, it does not view the Middle East as having vital "strategic" interests for China. Therefore, although it typically ascribes sinister motives to American actions in the region, it seeks to avoid confrontation with Washington over Middle East issues.

Balancing these two sets of interests—cooperation with countries in the region and relations with the United States—has required considerable restraint. Middle Eastern governments that Washington seeks to isolate often look to China as a potential savior and offer tempting trade opportunities. Many other Middle East states would welcome China's playing a more Soviet Union–like role in countering U.S. moves in the region, and playing to these sentiments would certainly give China a higher-profile role in the world. Meanwhile, Washington jealously guards its primacy in the region with friends and foes alike. From China's perspective this reeks of imperialism and arrogance.

As Beijing sees it, Washington is demanding that Chinese foreign policy toward the Middle East be based on U.S. interests and U.S. judgments, not on China's own. China does not have major conflicts of interest with Middle East countries; why should it forgo cooperation with them because the United States has conflicts? China's leaders have periodically debated the proper balance of conciliation and toughness in handling the United States. Their calculation about conciliating or rejecting U.S. Middle East demands could eventually shift in a more hard-line direction.

The United States could influence Beijing's Middle East calculus by seeking to expand China's access to Middle East resources in partnership with the United States—in exchange for greater Chinese support for U.S. efforts in the region. Washington might foster further Chinese involvement in the oil development of post-Saddam Iraq and even Saudi Arabia, building on commercial partnerships that are already under way. Such moves would encourage Beijing to view U.S. power in the Middle East in comport with, rather than being an obstacle to, China's quest for Middle East resources. They would provide incentives for China to expand Middle East diplomatic cooperation with the United States, perhaps even contributing to a more united front in regard to Iran's nuclear ambitions.

Such an approach would require a major shift in American thinking about China and the Middle East. There are also many reasons why Beijing might take whatever U.S. concessions were offered, while eschewing genuine partnership with the United States in the Middle East. But in an era in which both U.S. and Chinese involvement in the Middle East is deepening and in which a rising China and an incumbent paramount United States are struggling to work out an accommodation, Sino-American partnership in the Middle East might help shift relations onto a broadly cooperative and less conflictual course.

This chapter examines China's perception of the U.S. role in the Middle East, as well as its understanding of its own interests in the region. It then examines, in some detail, how China's balancing act—Beijing's attempts to expand multidimensional cooperation with Middle Eastern countries while maintaining good relations with Washington—has played out with respect to Iraq, Saudi Arabia, and Iran and attempts to derive some lessons from each case.

CHINA'S NARRATIVE OF THE U.S. DRIVE FOR
MIDDLE EASTERN HEGEMONY

A nearly universal belief in China is that U.S. policy in the Middle East is essentially about seizing control of that region's oil in order to coerce countries dependent on that oil, as part of a drive for global domination. Concerns about proliferation of weapons of mass destruction, terrorism, and democratization are seen as derivative or as pretexts for interventions directed at serving this objective. This view is expressed uniformly in Chinese newspaper commentary, scholarly articles published in China, and private interviews with Chinese analysts.

As long as the Soviet Union existed, the U.S. drive for hegemony in the Middle East was constrained by fear of Soviet intervention, according to the Chinese narrative. Confronted by a strong, confident, and ambitious regime in Moscow, Washington simply would not have dared to attack Iraq or other Soviet allies in the region. U.S. actions toward even the Middle Eastern countries not allied with Moscow— the Islamic Republic of Iran, for example—were constrained by fear of possible Soviet countermoves. The disintegration of the Soviet Union removed that constraint and resulted in an "extremely unbalanced" international system, with the United States no longer checked by a rival superpower. The result was an aggressive U.S. drive to bring the Middle East and its oil under full American sway in order to control the states that depended on that oil: Japan, India, the European countries, South Korea, and China. This would be a major step toward U.S. global domination.

The unconstrained U.S. drive to dominate the Middle East in the post-Soviet era began—again, in the Chinese view of things—with the decision in late 1990 to use military force to dislodge Iraqi forces from Kuwait. China condemned Iraq's invasion and annexation of Kuwait, but opposed international resort to military force to undo those moves.

The author of a March 1991 article in a publication of the Ministry of Foreign Affairs, *Shijie Zhishi (World Knowledge)*, maintained that the reason for the then recently concluded war to undo Iraq's occupation of Kuwait was "very simple": "The Gulf oil-producing countries export 90 percent of the crude oil they produce, mainly to the United States, Western Europe, and Japan." President George H.W. Bush's effort to "impose on the world a new order of his own choosing" was "a kind of new imperialism."[1]

Another author, writing in the same issue of *Shijie Zhishi*, elaborated on this conclusion: Iraq's occupation of Kuwait "presented . . . a favorable opportunity for the realization of a global strategy by the United States. The vast petroleum resources in the Gulf are of important strategic significance. Who controls the oil resources of this region controls the lifeblood of the world." The Soviets' decision to abandon their earlier policy of contending with the United States for control of the Middle East had given Washington an opportunity to use Iraq's move against Kuwait as an "opportunity to hit at Iraq." By controlling Persian Gulf oil and oil transport lines, the United States could "keep a tight rein on . . . rapidly rising allies like Germany and Japan."[2]

A document said to have been adopted at a meeting of the State Council and the General Office of the Chinese Communist Party (CCP) Central Committee in January 1991 reportedly determined the impending conflict between Iraq and a U.S.-led coalition to be a "struggle between global and regional hegemonies." The U.S. objectives were to "teach Saddam a lesson" and then "to dominate the world." Significantly, the document also indicated that China would refrain from openly criticizing "U.S. forces" and would maintain a neutral position in propaganda work "during the early stage of the conflict."[3]

Although Beijing professed to believe that economic sanctions would suffice to force Iraq to withdraw from Kuwait, China's leaders must have understood (as did virtually all Middle Eastern governments at the time) that the failure to use force to undo Iraq's move would result in the obliteration of the state of Kuwait. But Beijing apparently saw destruction of Kuwait as preferable to greater U.S. hegemony over Persian Gulf oil. From Beijing's viewpoint, Saddam Hussein's annexation of Kuwait was an "error" that pitted one third world country against another, thereby creating an opportunity for Washington to intensify its push for hegemony in the region.

Washington followed the 1991 war with an extensive sanctions regime designed to further weaken and subordinate Iraq. In 1993 the United States launched the policy of dual containment, unfolding more comprehensive sanctions against both Iraq and Iran. Sanctions against Iraq at least had UN authorization. This was not so in 1996 when American lawmakers enacted sanctions against all countries making certain investments in Iran and Libya. Beijing criticized these latter sanctions as "unilateral." It was also highly critical of the U.S. air strikes against Iraq starting in 1998.

Beijing saw the 2003 war to oust Saddam Hussein as merely another step in the United States' post–Cold War drive for Middle Eastern hegemony. A full-page commentary published on February 18, 2003, in *Huanqiu Shibao* (*Global Times*, a popular weekly paper published by *Renmin ribao*, the newspaper of the Central Committee of the Chinese Communist Party), and quoted the following day in *The Standard* of Hong Kong, is representative of the Chinese news media's coverage of the by-then looming war to oust Saddam. The United States had risen to a position of "global empire" through 200 years of constant "external expansion," of which the impending war was the culmination, it was explained. The first stage of this process involved continental expansion, the second stage overseas expansion, and the third a contest for global supremacy with Germany, Japan, and the Soviet Union. The fourth stage, now under way, entailed a post–Cold War effort to extend U.S. influence around the world.[4]

Prominent analysts in *Beijing Review* elaborated on the same theme. Ruan Zhongze, deputy director of the China Institute of International Studies, the Ministry of Foreign Affairs think tank, saw two major objectives behind the U.S. attack: to oust Saddam Hussein and "rebuild Iraq with a democratic system" in order to diminish the Middle East's production of terrorists; and "to establish U.S. oil hegemony." Chu Shulong, director of Tsinghua University's Institute of Strategic Studies, maintained that "oil is not the only reason the United States has attacked Iraq." Power per se was as important as oil. Chu explained:

> The attack is based on the desire to keep the Middle East from being dominated by an opponent and safeguard [U.S.] oil interests in the region. I believe that the major objective of the war is to topple the totalitarian rule of Saddam and thus dominate the Middle East . . . the United States has decided to control the region first by attacking Iraq.[5]

Li Guofu, a top Middle East expert at the Ministry of Foreign Affairs think tank, found that the main U.S. objective was to force Iraq into submission and warned that the next U.S. target would be Iran.[6]

A commentary in the People's Liberation Army newspaper *Jiefangjun Bao* in September 2002 linked the looming move against Iraq to growing U.S. military activity in Central Asia and Afghanistan. Washington was pursuing a "belt-shaped strategy" designed to dominate all of Eurasia, the author maintained. This putative U.S. strategy served three purposes. The first was to remove the "threat" posed to the United States by Iraq's possession of nuclear, biological, and chemical weapons. Second, Washington sought to control the oil resources of the Middle East:

> Iraq's oil will have a direct impact on the . . . world economy for the next 30 years, and [will be] an important tool to decide whether the United States can control the lifeline of the world economy. The United States has always regarded oil as the lifeline of itself and the entire capitalist world. If it can prop up a pro-U.S. government in Iraq, it can ensure undisturbed oil demand for a long time.[7]

The third U.S. strategic objective was to secure control over the oil transport routes from both the Persian Gulf and the Caspian Sea, according to the article. Regime change in Iraq would allow the United States to put more pressure on Iran and encroach more effectively on "the hinterland of the Eurasian continent." Control over Europe by means of NATO, over the Middle East by means of regime change in Iraq (and presumably Iran), plus domination of Asia and the Pacific "from Japan," would allow Washington to "dominate the entire world" as envisioned by Halford Mackinder, whose theory that Eurasia was the world's geopolitical pivot had "deeply influenced" U.S. global strategy, the article explained.

China perceived Washington's Broader Middle East and North Africa Initiative (BMENA) as equally sinister. The essential aim of BMENA, Beijing believed, was to create docile pro-U.S. states in the Middle East so as to bring that oil-rich region under firm U.S. control. China, by contrast, wanted efforts to reform the Middle East to be based on "mutual respect" and "equality," a Ministry of Foreign Affairs spokesman said.[8] *Huanqiu Shibao* carried an article titled "U.S. Grass Won't Grow on Arab Soil" explaining that the real goal of BMENA was control over the "plentiful oil resources" of the region. Washington wanted to "firmly grasp these resources."[9] Another analysis concluded that BMENA was a "major [U.S.] plot for the Middle East's future" and would lead to growing disputes between the United States and Middle Eastern countries. Arab countries considered the initiative "wanton interference in their destiny" and "rejected a uniform program imposed externally to transform the region with diversified conditions." Middle Eastern countries would "insist that the motivation for reform should come from inside, and any reform should follow local cultural, social, and religious conditions."[10]

Chinese analysts believe that American ambitions in the region will lead to a widening cycle of violence. They believe that the forces of U.S. hegemonism will continue to use war and sanctions in an attempt to bludgeon Middle Eastern nations into submission. They think U.S. efforts to impose Western political forms on the Middle East will undermine traditional institutions of state and social stability and predict these policies will produce a backlash that will lead to more terrorism.

Open Chinese criticism of U.S. Middle Eastern policies along the lines described above has typically not been strident. More often than not, explicit criticism of U.S. moves is put in the mouths of Middle Eastern actors. Terms of invective such as "hegemony" and "aggression" are used sparingly in open commentary—although they are more common in private discussions. Yet the underlying Chinese analysis was clear and virtually uniform: the United States is driving aggressively to bring the region under control for the sake of control of its oil and ultimately world domination.

WATCHING THE TIGERS FIGHT

The dire analysis of U.S. imperialism run amok in the Middle East has *not* determined the Chinese policy response to U.S. policies. There is an extremely important disjuncture between the anti-hegemony narrative prevalent in China and repeated decisions by Beijing to avoid standing too closely with the anti-hegemonic forces in the region.

Although Beijing has often provided sympathy and low-key support to indigenous efforts to foil U.S. foreign policy in the Middle East, it has been markedly reluctant to offer overt or high-level assistance. Moreover, in response to U.S. demands, China has repeatedly disengaged from various types of cooperation with Middle Eastern states. Time and again Beijing has shown itself willing to trade lower levels of Chinese opposition to U.S. moves for U.S. concessions on other issues important to China. "Sitting on the mountain, watching the tigers fight" is an ancient Chinese stratagem that perhaps fairly characterizes China's approach to U.S. policy in the Middle East.

Partly this is because the Chinese tend to believe that the grandiose ambitions of the United States to control the Middle East and its oil will not succeed in any case. Chinese analysts, and very probably the leaders they advise, are convinced that hegemonic U.S. designs in the

Middle East will eventually fail, even without China's active support for the anti-hegemonic forces, because of intrinsic weaknesses in U.S. policy.

In a November 2004 article in *China Daily*, foreign policy veteran Qian Qichen argued that the U.S. strategy of aggressive preemptive war would ultimately lead to the demise of the "American empire." The U.S. predicament in Iraq, Qian said, reflected a "superiority psychology [that] inflates beyond its real capability," causing a lot of trouble. The "cocksureness and arrogance" of U.S. policy in Iraq had "made the United States even more unpopular in the international community than [during] its war in Vietnam" and had "destroyed the hard-won global anti-terror coalition." Furthermore, U.S. policy had widened the rift between the United States and Europe: "It is now time to give up the illusion that Europeans and Americans are living in the same world, as some Europeans would like to believe," Qian wrote.[11]

According to Chinese commentary, U.S. plans to dominate the Middle East will be defeated by the resistance of the peoples and governments of that region. Another factor in the U.S. failure will be the Americans' ethnocentric ignorance and arrogance—the naive belief that the United States can impose Western values and institutions on Arab and Persian Muslim peoples with patterns of historical development much different from those of the West. Nor will the resources of the United States prove adequate to subordinate the Middle East; the quest will be too expensive in money and blood. The American people will not have the stomach for what is demanded. Eventually, the peoples and nations of the Middle East will emerge to independently shape their own destinies. Obviously, this is a politically correct "happy ending" to China's hegemony narrative. But there is also ample evidence that it is actually part of China's belief system.

"The Middle East is a graveyard of great powers": this was a theme sounded repeatedly by different Chinese analysts in the authors' discussions in early 2007 in Beijing. Britain and France in the Levant in 1956 and earlier, the Soviet Union in Afghanistan in the 1980s, and the United States in Iraq starting in 2003 all encountered costly and humiliating setbacks in the region, we were told. A former ambassador to Iran told us that the deepening American quagmire in Iraq constituted a warning to China to avoid deep involvement in the Middle East.

The Middle East is extremely complex and complicated, and difficult to understand, Chinese analysts told us. One prominent analyst said that the strong role of religion in Middle Eastern politics is incomprehensible to China, a country ruled by atheists where religion has "never held political power."

Furthermore, the unanimous view was that China has no vital "strategic" interests in the Middle East requiring protection. The region is distant from China and is not an area from which hostile forces might threaten China's territory. Nor is it a traditional Chinese sphere of influence. China's interests in the Middle East are mainly commercial: oil and trade. China intends to pursue friendly, cooperative relations with all Middle Eastern countries on behalf of these interests, but does not consider them worth the risks and other costs associated with entanglement in Middle Eastern conflicts.

China does have an interest in maintaining stability in the Middle East, but direct involvement in that region in pursuit of this interest is beyond Chinese capabilities, we were repeatedly told. China hopes that the United States will uphold stability in the Middle East, and Beijing is willing to cooperate with Washington in that regard to the extent that China's limited capabilities allow. Regarding U.S. military deployments and even interventions in the Middle East, China cannot openly support such actions. However, it recognizes that military moves by the United States in that region often serve China's interests and thus does not seriously oppose U.S. efforts. Several Chinese analysts frankly stated that China intends to "free ride" on U.S. efforts in the Middle East. But if U.S. efforts to stabilize the Middle East fail (perhaps because of inadequate support from China and other countries), China will not step in. In such a situation, if the Middle East threatens to slip into chaos, China hopes that someone else will intervene—Europe, Russia, the United Nations, even Iran. It would not really matter who, one analyst said.

If China's efforts at energy cooperation with Middle Eastern countries fail, or if conditions in the region degenerate into chaos, China will "go elsewhere" for oil, to Africa or Latin America. Conservation, increased efficiency, and the development of cleaner-burning coal and nonfossil fuels will also help. These solutions may cost more, but will ultimately be less costly than Middle Eastern adventures and possible diplomatic humiliations and will allow China to retain greater control of its foreign involvements.

The Chinese calculation also seems to be that opposition to U.S. policy in the Middle East would be too costly in terms of broader U.S.-

China relations. The United States is an arrogant, hegemonic power seeking to control Middle Eastern oil as a stepping-stone to world domination. But precisely *because* the Middle East is the focus of this alleged drive for world domination, Chinese efforts to counter the United States in that region could easily spoil Sino-American comity, thereby undermining the favorable international climate for China's development drive.

Achievement of "national wealth and power" (*fuguo qiangbing* in Chinese) has been the overall objective of Chinese patriots since the late nineteenth century. In 1978 under the leadership of Deng Xiaoping, China adopted a new approach to achieving this: bold and deepening integration into global markets based on the free flow of goods, capital, technology, information, and people. Deng and the Chinese leaders who followed him understood that, for better or worse, the United States dominated the global economic system and that if China hoped to follow the path of earlier East Asian globalizing developmental states (Japan, South Korea, Taiwan, Singapore), it should strive to maintain comity with the United States.

Thus far Beijing has ranked maintenance of Sino-American comity above expanded cooperation with Middle East states. When Beijing has deemed it necessary to safeguard Beijing's relation with the United States, China has halted, limited, slowed—and at other times hidden and denied—Middle East cooperation deemed objectionable by Washington. This has happened repeatedly, although often not without equivocation, or not without a quid pro quo from Washington.

CHINA'S MIDDLE EASTERN POLICIES AND INTERESTS

Along with relations with the United States, there are two key dimensions to China's emerging political role in the Middle East: (1) expanding friendly, multidimensional cooperation and relations of mutual understanding and trust with *all* countries in the region, which entails maintaining a degree of neutrality and evenhandedness in conflicts between Middle Eastern states; (2) channeling Middle Eastern resources—export markets, capital, and, above all, petroleum—into China's development drive. To secure access to petroleum resources in the event of crises, Beijing seeks to encapsulate energy supply relations in political relations valuable to the supplier.

Beijing's omni-directional friendship policy in the Middle East took shape early in the rule of Deng Xiaoping (1978–1997), with China's declaration of neutrality at the onset of the Iran-Iraq War (1980–1988). China succeeded in maintaining cordial relations with Iraq during the war, even while emerging as Iran's major arms supplier, nuclear partner, and supporter in the United Nations Security Council. Omni-directionality continued during the 1990s, when China forged normal and even cooperative relations with Israel—the two countries established full diplomatic ties in 1992—while continuing its friendship with the Palestinian Liberation Organization and later the Palestinian Authority as well as rejectionist states such as Iran, Syria, and Iraq. Following the onset in 2003 of the U.S.-led war in Iraq and the concurrent growth of regional hegemonic competition between Iran and Saudi Arabia, China again showed its ability to remain neutral, developing friendly, cooperative relations with both Tehran and Riyadh.

It is widely believed in the United States that China supports anti-U.S. governments in the Middle East. That belief is only half true. The People's Republic of China has a history of seeking greater friendship and cooperation with Middle Eastern states that enjoy friendly relations with the United States (Saudi Arabia, Jordan, the small Persian Gulf states, Egypt, Israel) as well as states in the region that are or have been locked in conflict with the United States (the Islamic Republic of Iran, Iraq under Saddam Hussein, Syria, Libya prior to 2002). Basically, China seeks multidimensional cooperative relations with *all* governments in the Middle East, especially those ruling the more powerful nations in the region, regardless of the condition of those governments' relations with the United States.

China's "principled stance" is that no basic conflict of interest exists between China and any country of the Middle East and that cooperation between China and Middle Eastern countries should not be held hostage to U.S. conflicts with those countries. Although U.S. representatives may package their arguments for Chinese nonassociation with rivals of the United States in terms of respect for global norms and institutions, Beijing believes that, at bottom, the actual proposition is that China should have nothing to do with countries on the outs with Washington. But in the view of the Chinese, this would transform their country into a vassal of the United States.

Principle aside, the reality of conflict between the United States and Middle Eastern states has created important opportunities for Chinese diplomacy, particularly in Iraq under Saddam Hussein and Iran. Since September 11, 2001, a similar dynamic has developed with Saudi Arabia. Yet even as it has effectively pursued these opportunities, China

Figure 2.1. China's Petroleum Production and Consumption

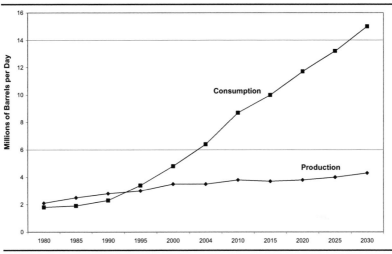

Source: Data from the U.S. Energy Information Administration. Historical and current: see Table 1.2 World Petroleum Consumption, 1980–2005, available at http://www.eia.doe.gov/ pub/international/iealf/table12.xls, and Table 2.2 World Crude Oil Production, 1980–2005, available at http://www.eia.doe.gov/pub/international/iealf/table22.xls. Future projections: see *International Energy Outlook 2006,* Table E1. World Oil Production Capacity by Region and Country, Reference Case, 1990–2030, and Table A4. World Oil Consumption by Region, Reference Case, 1990–2030, available at http://www.eia.doe.gov/oiaf/ieo/pdf/0484(2006).pdf.

has been quite pragmatic in balancing the relatively modest goals they represent with its fundamental interest in maintaining cordial relations with the United States.

SUSTAINING CHINA'S SUCCESSFUL DEVELOPMENT DRIVE

At the heart of Beijing's interest in the Middle East in the early twenty-first century is the desire for an uninterrupted flow of oil to China to sustain the country's booming economy. According to the International Energy Administration, in 2004 China produced about 54 percent of the oil it consumed. The rest was imported. China's energy shortfall is projected to grow rapidly, as illustrated by figure 2.1. Chinese analysts note that countries that industrialized in earlier periods enjoyed an energy-abundant environment that no longer exists. Energy shortfalls could hobble China's development, and a high Chinese priority is to ensure that that does not happen by keeping adequate supplies of foreign oil flowing to China.

China's unexpected demand growth in 2004 transformed the global oil market. Demand growth in 2004 was double the average of the previous decade and ate away at remaining spare capacity, tightening

Figure 2.2. China's Middle East Trade as a Percent of China's Global Trade

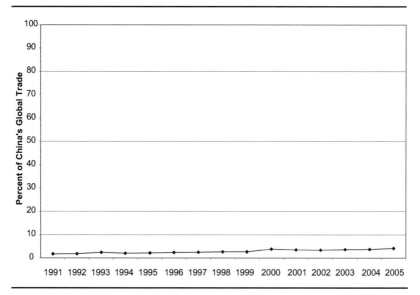

Source: China statistical yearbooks, various years.

Figure 2.3. Regional Destinations of Chinese Outward-bound Foreign Direct Investment, 2003–2004

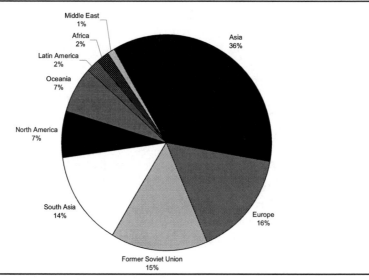

Source: Philip C. Saunders, *China's Global Activism: Strategy, Drivers, and Tools,* Occasional Paper no. 4 (Washington, D.C.: National Defense University, Institute for National Strategic Studies, October 2006), 20, 50.

markets and allowing prices to move significantly with small disruptions and tension.

China's exports of goods and services to the oil-based economies of the Middle East are the flip side of its energy imports from that region and have also expanded rapidly. The Middle Eastern oil states are major consumers of Chinese light manufactured goods, machinery and equipment, vehicles, foodstuffs, and engineering and labor services. Many of these states are placing increased stress on all-around economic development and see Chinese goods and services as economically and politically attractive. Chinese goods and post-sale services are typically cheap. Nor does Chinese cooperation come with the "interference in internal affairs" that is so common with Western cooperation.

The same upheavals that drew the United States ever more deeply into the Middle East—the Iranian revolution, the Iran-Iraq War, Iraq and Iran's pariah status—have created commercial opportunities for China. Opportunities have opened to Chinese firms especially when Western firms faced legal or other obstacles to commercial interactions in certain countries.

However, it is important to keep China's Middle Eastern trade, including oil imports, in perspective. The value of China's Middle Eastern trade, including oil imports, constitutes a small percentage of China's global trade (see figure 2.2). In 2005, for instance, China's total two-way trade with Saudi Arabia, then its number one oil supplier, represented 7.6 percent of two-way China-U.S. trade, 8.7 percent of China–Japan trade, and 1.1 percent of China's total exports and imports.[12] China's two-way trade with all Middle Eastern and North African countries—including Chinese oil imports—accounted in 2005 for only 4.2 percent of its global trade. There is a steady but gradual growth in Sino–Middle Eastern trade; but China's global trade is simply so great that the entire Middle Eastern region still plays a relatively minor role.

It is also important to keep in mind that China's vast global trade, together with its $1.33 trillion in foreign currency reserves (as of June 2007), gives it considerable financial wherewithal to respond to jumps in oil prices linked to Middle Eastern crises. This is yet another reason it can avoid undue entanglement in the region.

In terms of Chinese investment, the Middle East ranks last among the regions of the world. In 2004, the region accounted for 1 percent of China's investment abroad (figure 2.3). This reflects both the difficulties and the risks of doing business in the Middle East and China's efforts to diversify its oil supply away from disproportionate dependence on Middle Eastern sources. Table 2.1 shows Chinese energy relationships with Middle Eastern and North African countries.

CONSTRUCTIVE ENGAGEMENT WITH THE UNITED STATES IN IRAQ

The U.S. campaigns against Saddam Hussein provide many instances of China's avoidance of confrontation with Washington over the Middle East. It also provides examples of how China's restraint in opposing U.S. actions in the region sometimes requires a quid pro quo from Washington. Most recently, Iraq shows how the United States might include China as a constructive partner in the region in a way that furthers the interests of both powers (as well as the people of the Middle East).

The first round of U.S.-PRC bargaining over Iraq occurred in late 1990, when Beijing was still suffering under U.S. sanctions resulting from the June 1989 massacre in Beijing, and Washington, for its part, ardently desired UN Security Council authorization for military action to roll back Iraq's annexation of Kuwait. U.S. lobbying for Chinese support began the afternoon of the very day Iraqi forces moved into Kuwait and continued over the following weeks. In Cairo in November 1990, Secretary of State James Baker explored with Foreign Minister Qian Qichen what might be necessary to secure Chinese support or at least acquiescence regarding Security Council authorization of military action to oust Iraq from Kuwait. In Qian's view, Washington's need for Chinese cooperation was an "advantageous opportunity" to restore normal U.S.-China relations, and Qian indicated to Baker that China would at least not veto a U.S. proposal for military action if Washington promised to find a politically convenient opportunity to lift the sanctions imposed on China in 1989. China abstained on Security Council Resolution 678, which authorized the use of force against Iraq. Before the vote, Baker had asked China to vote "yes" rather then merely abstain on the resolution, but Qian saw this request as a U.S. effort to "raise the price" after it had already been agreed on.[13]

Following the UN cease-fire resolution of April 1991, China began arguing that continued sanctions harmed the people of Iraq and should be lifted as quickly as possible, putting it in opposition to U.S. efforts to maintain them. By the end of the 1990s, China was supporting an intensified effort by France and Russia to end sanctions against

Table 2.1. Chinese Investments and Energy Ties with Middle Eastern and North African Countries

Date	Country	PRC Company	Description
1997	Iraq	CNPC	22-year production-sharing agreement and development of al-Ahdab field, value estimated at $1.3 billion; suspended by 2003 war
1998	Egypt	CNPC	Agreement with 2 Egyptian companies to set up joint investment company
2001	Iran	Sinopec	$150-million deal to design and build oil-unloading terminal at Neka and modernize refineries at Rey and Tabris; part of CROS project
2003	Algeria	CNPC	Agreement to invest $31 million over 3 years in prospecting for oil and gas
2004	Saudi Arabia	Sinopec	Gas exploration and production agreement w/ Saudi Aramco, valued at $300 million
2004	Egypt	Petrochina	Petroleum investment agreement
2004	Algeria	CNPC & Sinopec	Grant of 3 exploration blocks
2004	Libya	PRC government	Agreement to purchase 10 million barrels of oil, value estimated at $300 million
2004	Iran	Sinopec	MOU to purchase 10 million tons of LNG a year, over 25 years, for lead role in Yadavaran development; $2 billion contract for 1st phase signed in December 2007
2004	Saudi Arabia (in Fujian province)	Sinopec	Agreement to upgrade and triple capacity of Quanzhou refinery in cooperation w/ Saudi Aramco and ExxonMobil, valued at $3.5 billion; ground broken July 2005
2006	Saudi Arabia (in Hainan province)	governments	Agreement to set up 10-million-cubic-meter-oil storage facility on Hainan Island
2007	Iraq	CNPC	Reconfirmation of 1997 deal to develop al-Ahdab field in exchange for Chinese cancellation of large portion of Iraqi debt to China
2007	Iran	CNOOC	Agreement on upstream and downstream development of North Pars natural gas field

Source: John W. Garver.

Figure 2.4. War, Sanctions, and Iraqi Oil Exports to China

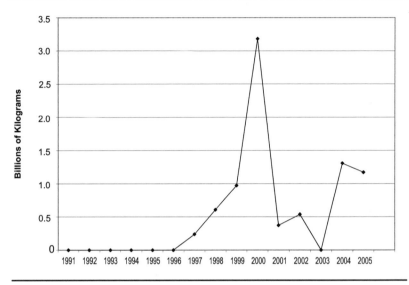

Source: Zhongguo haiguan tongji nianjian [China customs statistical yearbook] (Beijing: Chinese Customs Statistical Bureau, various years).

Figure 2.5. Oil-for-Food Sales by Buyer Country of Registration

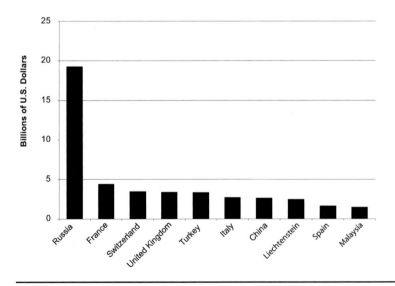

Source: Independent Inquiry Committee into the United Nations Oil-for-Food Programme, "Briefing Paper," October 21, 2004, Appendix table 3, available at http://www.iic-offp.org/documents/ IIC%20Tables%2010-21-2004.pdf.

Iraq. Sanctions on Iraq also interfered with Chinese procurement of Iraqi oil—a situation illustrated by figure 2.4.

Beijing was nonetheless very cautious when it came to violating these sanctions. When Iraq reopened the Baghdad airport in August 2000, in defiance of a 1990 UN ban on air traffic with Iraq, a number of countries proceeded to send planes into Baghdad including Russia, France, Jordan, Syria, Egypt, and Bulgaria. Only in December, after those six other countries, which included two of the Security Council's Permanent Five, had sent flights into Baghdad, did China do so.[14]

Starting at the end of 1996, the Oil-for-Food (OFF) Program greatly expanded oil sales permitted under the terms of the 1991 cease-fire by allowing Iraq to sell oil to customers it selected itself, with funds from those sales going into an account that it could use to import humanitarian goods. During the first three years of the program, China's role on the Security Council plus its opposition to the continuation of sanctions made it a favorite of Iraqi officials, and thus the third-largest recipient of OFF oil. In 2000, however, Iraq began demanding kickbacks. China-registered firms were apparently unwilling to make the demanded payments, though firms of other countries were. As a result, other countries surpassed China during the last three years of the program. In terms of overall purchases of Iraqi allocations of oil under OFF, China ranked only seventh, behind, among others, Italy, Turkey, and the United Kingdom, as shown in figure 2.5.

Similarly, in terms of providing humanitarian goods under OFF, China ended up ranked eighth, supplying only about 5 percent of such goods (see figure 2.6) procured by the Iraqi government.

Foreign-based affiliates of Chinese firms were, however, willing to make the demanded kickback payments. If purchases by foreign-registered affiliates of Chinese firms are credited to China, then China surpasses France to become the second-largest purchaser of OFF oil (though still at a level far below that of Russia). The London-based affiliate of Sinochem (one of China's largest chemical producers), for example, was the second-largest oil purchaser under OFF, receiving nearly $2.2 billion (3.4 percent) of total Iraqi oil allocations of $64.2 billion under the program.

It is not clear whether the large purchases of OFF oil by Sinochem-London was an arrangement authorized by Beijing, or a practice beyond Beijing's control. But either way, Beijing seems to have been acting to keep distance between itself and the use of OFF to acquire Iraqi oil. In spite of China's opposition in the Security Council to continuation

Figure 2.6. Suppliers of Humanitarian Goods to Iraq under OFF Program, 1997–2003

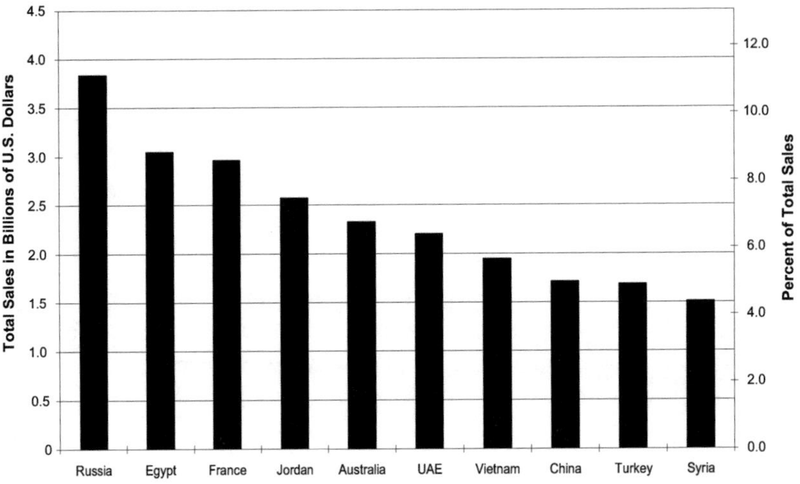

Source: Independent Inquiry Committee into the United Nations Oil-for-Food Programme, *Manipulation of the Oil-for-Food Programme by the Iraqi Regime,* October 27, 2005, 262, available at http://www.iic-offp.org/documents/IIC%20Final%20Report%2027Oct2005.pdf.

of the sanctions regime, China did not rush into the open door offered by OFF. There is a stark contrast here between the behavior of China and that of Russia and France. Although China needed Iraqi oil, it pursued it in a cautious, low-profile fashion and not at the cost of becoming seen in international, and especially American eyes, as a patron of Saddam Hussein.

Another example of Chinese restraint came in 2001, when the United States demanded that China suspend involvement in the construction of a fiber-optic cable network in Iraq. U.S. and British anti-radar missiles had been highly effective over the previous several years at destroying Iraqi radar sites that "locked on" to U.S. Air Force and Royal Air Force aircraft operating in the no-fly zone over southern Iraq. Baghdad responded by attempting to build a fiber-optic network that would link missile batteries in southern Iraq to radars near Baghdad and thus outside the no-fly zone. The United States protested China's role at a high level; the objections included remarks by President George W. Bush to the Chinese ambassador during their first meeting in the White House, early in 2001. Beijing initially rejected U.S. charges, then promised a "serious investigation." After that investigation, Foreign Minister Tang

Jiaxuan denied that Chinese firms had helped Iraq strengthen its air defenses. Privately, however, Beijing informed Washington that Chinese firms had been ordered to cease such activities in Iraq.[15]

Beijing had condemned Washington's policies of no-fly zones and air strikes against Iraq. Yet, confronted by a U.S. demand to cease undermining the no-fly zone, Beijing quietly suspended involvement in the fiber-optic cable project. A few months later, Beijing agreed with Washington not to veto a U.S. push at the Security Council for "smart sanctions" (whereby import of UN supervised civilian goods by Iraq would become easier, while stricter safeguards would be implemented to check smuggling of oil out of and civilian goods into Iraq) in exchange for U.S. release of $80 million in frozen Iraqi funds to pay for dual-use telecommunications equipment shipped by China to Iraq.[16]

China's response in late 2002 to Washington's push for UN approval of a war to remove Saddam Hussein—which culminated on November 8 with Security Council Resolution 1441—offers a further example of China's policy of restraint. France, Russia, and Germany at that juncture voiced strong opposition to the U.S. push for war. China also explicitly and repeatedly expressed disapproval of U.S. war plans, but China's statements of opposition during Security Council debates were less sharp, far less verbose, and less frequent and came later in the debates. China was careful to keep its opposition to U.S. moves several steps behind that of France, Russia, and Germany. Beijing supported the Franco-Russian call for the return of UN inspectors to Iraq and made clear its opposition to a U.S. resort to military force, especially force not authorized by the Security Council. But in late September, China indicated that it was willing to study any U.S. draft resolution submitted to the Security Council, thereby breaking ranks with Moscow, Paris, and Berlin, all of which were insisting that a resolution was unnecessary until UN inspectors returned to Iraq and found that it had failed to meet its obligations.[17] China's shift helped move the Security Council toward Resolution 1441.

President Bush discussed Iraq with Jiang Zemin during their talks at Bush's Crawford, Texas, ranch in late October 2002. An anonymous "senior administration official" afterward told the press that, regarding the Bush-Jiang discussions of Iraq, "We have a lot of common ground with the Chinese. We think we're working well with them on this."[18] Resolution 1441 passed the Security Council in a form ambiguous enough to allow Washington to find in it a degree of authorization for military action against Iraq should Saddam Hussein fail to comply with a final set of Security Council demands.

When Resolution 1441 passed, Beijing joined with Russia and France to issue a joint statement asserting opposition to military action by the United States.[19] Yet four months later, in March 2003, when U.S.-led military action against Iraq was imminent, China declined to again join with Russia, France, and Germany when those three states drafted another joint statement of opposition to the impending U.S. attack.[20] According to Chinese analysts interviewed in early 2007, during the Security Council debates over Iraq, France asked China to speak more forcefully in opposition to U.S. moves, but China demurred. According to another Chinese analyst interviewed during Secretary of State Colin Powell's February 2003 visit to Beijing to seek Chinese support in the Security Council, Iraq was not worth a setback in the post–9/11 warming trend in U.S.-China relations.

Still another manifestation of Beijing's policy of restraint in opposing the 2003 U.S. invasion of Iraq was the absence of mass antiwar, anti-U.S. demonstrations in the weeks preceding the invasion. As the Hong Kong newspaper *Hsin Pao* pointed out, "By not allowing the people to march in the street, and by suppressing anti-U.S. sentiment, the Chinese government was doing the United States a favor."[21]

As in 1990, there was a quid pro quo for Chinese cooperation in 2002–2003. Once again Washington needed Chinese support in the Security Council, and again Beijing used the opportunity to secure U.S. concessions on other issues: in this case, designation of the East Turkestan Independence Movement (ETIM) as a terrorist organization and (reportedly) prevention of a U.S. military strike against North Korea's nuclear facilities. Regarding ETIM, ever since the 9/11 attacks on the United States, Beijing had sought to secure Washington's understanding for China's own fight against terrorism, including against Uighur separatists from Xinjiang grouped around ETIM. China was willing to support U.S. efforts against al Qaeda but insisted that "there should be no double standard."[22] For more than a year, Washington rejected Beijing's demand that it treat ETIM as a terrorist organization. Then, in August 2002, as the Bush administration moved toward finalizing its decision to go to war to remove Saddam Hussein, the U.S. position on ETIM changed.[23] Deputy Secretary of State Richard Armitage visited China late that month to discuss Iraq. The day before Armitage met with Hu Jintao, the State Department added ETIM to the U.S. list of terrorist organizations.

A second round of bargaining involving North Korea apparently transpired in February 2003, when Secretary of State Powell visited Beijing in an effort to persuade China not to insist on a second Security Council resolution authorizing the use of force against Iraq, or otherwise use its Security Council veto to block the imminent U.S. attack. During Powell's visit, Beijing reportedly agreed not to attempt to block a U.S. war against Iraq in exchange for a U.S. agreement not to attack North Korea's nuclear facilities—an example of Beijing's trading diminished Chinese opposition to U.S. moves in the Middle East for U.S. concessions on issues important to China. A Chinese official was the source of the leak of this information.[24]

Once Saddam Hussein was removed, China played a role in persuading Russia, France, and Germany to join in a Security Council resolution giving a UN imprimatur to U.S. leadership of Iraq's reconstruction. The thrust of China's arguments to these other powers was suggested by Beijing's ambassador to the United Nations, Wang Guangya: "You have to recognize that the U.S. is the biggest country in the world. If they do not want to participate in the UN, I don't think the UN will work effectively."[25]

A benevolent U.S. attitude toward China's efforts to acquire Iraqi oil after Saddam Hussein's ouster paralleled China's relatively supportive attitude for U.S. efforts in post-Saddam Iraq. China's large-scale involvement in Middle Eastern upstream oil development began in June 1997, when the China National Petroleum Corporation (CNPC) signed a $1.2 billion agreement with Iraq's national oil company to jointly develop a rich new field in southern Iraq, al-Ahdab, with an expected production of 90,000 barrels a day (bbl/d). To some extent, the agreement with CNPC was a reward for China's ongoing opposition to the continuation of economic sanctions against Iraq. Work on the al-Ahdab field was suspended when China withdrew its personnel from Iraq in the run-up to the March 2003 invasion. The subsequent ouster of Saddam Hussein's regime cast the 1997 agreement into limbo, with Iraq's interim government declaring its intention to review all oil deals signed during Saddam's rule.

The new Iraqi government constituted in 2006 began negotiations with China in November of that year on reviving the agreement. Significantly, the 1997 al-Ahdab agreement with China was the first accord with a foreign oil firm taken up for renegotiation by the new government. Iraqi leaders believed that China, with its experience operating in dangerous places such as Sudan and Angola, would be less concerned than Western oil firms about the security risks associated with operating in Iraq.

Negotiations to resuscitate the al-Ahdab deal became linked to cancellation of all or part of an $8 billion debt owed to China by Iraq. Meanwhile, CNPC developed a detailed new development plan for al-Ahdab in line with the specifications of the new Iraqi government. The two states achieved a breakthrough during Iraqi president Jalal Talabani's visit to China in May 2007—the first to China by an Iraqi president since diplomatic relations were established in 1958. During Talabani's stay, China canceled Iraqi debt owed to the Chinese central government, and China's leading role in al-Ahdab's development was reconfirmed in a new agreement.[26]

The United States has an interest in involving more countries—especially powerful states such as China—in the reconstruction of post-Saddam Iraq. Yet Washington is unlikely to be sympathetic to resumption of Chinese development of al-Ahdab if China is perceived as hostile to U.S. policies in the Middle East. China's participation in Iraqi oil development projects is facilitated by a benign American view of China's role in that region.

During interviews in Beijing in early 2007, the authors of the present volume encountered strong suspicion that the Iraqi oil law then being drafted would give British and American oil firms a monopoly over Iraq's oil. By using its influence with the new Iraqi government to revive the 1997 deal and involve China in Iraqi oil development, Washington rewarded Beijing for its relatively low-key opposition to U.S. policies in Iraq.

THE NEW SINO-SAUDI RELATIONSHIP

China's initial efforts at oil development cooperation with Iraq (and Iran—as described below) involved collaboration with a state caught up in confrontation with the United States. It was a different case with Saudi Arabia, a close U.S. ally of long standing.

But even with Saudi Arabia, the Chinese have sometimes found their bilateral partnership in stark conflict with American interests. The most prominent example was China's sale of intermediate-range, nuclear-capable ballistic missiles to Saudi Arabia first revealed in 1988. The sale of the CSS-2 missiles led to strong U.S. protests. The missiles have a range of more than 1,500 miles and can carry a payload of more than 4,000 lbs. After a period of resistance to U.S. demands, Beijing finally agreed to end such sales,[27] and no further sales were reported.[28] Once again China maneuvered to minimize conflict with the United States over Middle East issues. As the CSS-2 missiles approach the end of their life cycle, however, there is speculation that Saudi Arabia seeks to upgrade its ballistic missile capacity and possibly move to the solid-fuel CSS-5 or CSS-6 as opposed to its existing liquid-fuel missiles.[29]

The Beijing-Riyadh relation started to grow more robust in the late 1990s, as Saudi Arabia began pushing to diversify its economy and China intensified its search for oil. Since then, Sino-Saudi energy relations have expanded rapidly. A comment in 2006 by the New China News Agency well summarized Beijing's view of the emerging Sino-Saudi relationship: "Saudi Arabia is a very good and reliable oil supplier. It is not like Nigeria, which is so fraught with uncertain factors that its oil supply fluctuates sharply. Neither is it like Iraq and Iran, whose oil supply was affected by unstable political situations."[30]

In 2004, Sinopec (China's second-largest oil firm, after CNPC) joined with Saudi Aramco and the American firm ExxonMobil to undertake a $3.5 billion refinery complex at Quanzhou in Fujian Province, tripling its refining capacity and allowing it to process "distressed" Saudi crude. The project was a win-win enterprise, giving China long-term supply and Saudi Arabia an outlet for "distressed" crude, which has fewer buyers. In 2005 Aramco joined with Sinopec to undertake development of the large, new natural gas field at Rub al Khali. In 2006, the two sides agreed to jointly build an oil storage facility capable of holding 62.9 million barrels of oil (10 million cubic meters) on the Chinese island of Hainan adjacent to an economic development zone where Sinopec was building an oil refinery. Saudi Arabia also invited Chinese firms to participate in infrastructure developments worth $624 billion.[31] From both the Saudi and Chinese perspectives, the deals made sense, and Saudi oil minister Ali Naimi has remarked that Asia is the logical market for the Middle East.

Although economics is the crux of the new Sino-Saudi relationship, relations took on a new political dimension after the 9/11 attacks as strains emerged in U.S.-Saudi relations over Saudi nationals' involvement in international terrorism. Saudi leaders viewed ties to China as a hedge against deepening tensions in the Saudi-U.S. relationship—and greatly appreciated Beijing's policy of strict noninterference in Saudi Arabia's internal affairs, which contrasted with Washington's drive for greater political reform in the region. Riyadh and Beijing increasingly discussed political issues and found a meeting of the minds on such issues as Iraq, the Iran nuclear issue, the penchant of the United States and other Western countries to interfere in other states' internal affairs, and the role of the United Nations.[32]

From a U.S. foreign policy perspective, perhaps the most important factor in the post–9/11 Sino-Saudi political relationship is both states' fear that U.S. moves under President George W. Bush would lead to greater instability in the Middle East. In October 2002, as Washington was pushing the UN Security Council to sanction the use of force should Saddam Hussein's regime fail one final test regarding full cooperation with UN weapons inspectors, Chinese deputy foreign minister Yang Wenchang flew to Riyadh to discuss the Iraq situation. Yang told Saudi leaders that China opposed the use of military force against Iraq and felt that issues relating to Iraq should be settled by political and diplomatic means within the framework of the United Nations. The last proviso implied opposition to U.S. moves against Iraq without UN authorization. The pressing task of the moment, Yang said, was to have UN arms inspectors return to Iraq as soon as possible, and for Iraq to unconditionally and comprehensively implement its obligations under relevant UN resolutions.[33] When UN arms inspectors reentered Iraq late in 2002, two specialists from the Chinese government were among them. After hearing Yang's presentation of China's position, Abdallah, then Saudi crown prince, expressed appreciation for China's stance on the Iraq issue and thanked China for upholding justice. China was one of the closest friends of Saudi Arabia, Abdallah said.[34]

Following the April 2003 ouster of Saddam Hussein, and as Washington and London were pushing for UN endorsement of allied occupation of Iraq, Beijing and Riyadh again coordinated policies, this time by means of telephone discussions between their respective foreign ministers. The two sides agreed that the Iraq issue should be "handled in accordance with the spirit of the UN Charter," with the Security Council playing a key role, and with regional peace and stability in mind. Foreign Minister Li Zhaoxing also said that China would increase humanitarian assistance to the Iraqi people and would cooperate with other parties, including Saudi Arabia, to "take an active part in Iraq's postwar reconstruction."[35] Although the contents of this exchange were anodyne, it is significant that the two sides were talking and striving to work in parallel on the issue of war and peace in Iraq.

Riyadh and Beijing both quickly lined up in opposition to the U.S. effort to democratize the Middle East by means of the Broader Middle

East and North Africa Initiative, endorsed by the Group of Eight (G-8) in June 2004. Both capitals saw BMENA as unwarranted interference in the domestic politics of other countries, as U.S. ethnocentric arrogance, and, worst of all, as an incitement to greater extremism and instability in the region. In September 2004, Beijing and Riyadh signed an agreement arranging for regular political consultations. A senior Chinese diplomat explained that "the two countries will support each other on international issues."[36]

In January 2006, Abdallah, having recently been named king, made what president (since 2003) and CCP paramount leader Hu Jintao pointed out was a "three firsts" visit to China: (1) the first-ever visit by a Saudi monarch to China, (2) China's status as the first country visited by King Abdallah as king, and (3) China's position as first stop on the king's multi-country tour. These symbolized, Hu said, the growing closeness of Sino-Saudi ties. A mere three months after Abdallah's visit, Hu came to Riyadh in the course of a six-nation tour. During Hu's visit, five agreements for expanded cooperation were signed, including one on oil, gas, and mineral cooperation, and another on economics, trade, and technological cooperation.

When receiving Hu, King Abdallah urged China to pay more attention to Middle Eastern issues.[37] President Hu laid a four-point proposal before Abdallah for enhancing Sino-Saudi relations. The first point called for the two countries to support each other in their efforts to safeguard national sovereignty and territorial integrity and to continue strengthening mutual support and cooperation on international and regional affairs. This statement implicitly targeted U.S. efforts to democratize the Middle East by such means as regime change in Iraq and BMENA.[38]

Underlying the new Sino-Saudi political partnership is opposition to Western and especially U.S. insistence on global political norms. The CCP and the Saudi monarchy both feel threatened by such pressure. Both the CCP and the Saudi monarchy have little use for elections, and both feel that they must maintain tight state control over the media, the Internet, and civil society for the sake of political and social stability. Beijing and Riyadh agree that whatever reforms are necessary must proceed in a manner acceptable to the governments of the sovereign countries involved. During his visit to Riyadh in 1999, then president Jiang Zemin stated the Sino-Saudi consensus rebutting the U.S. position: "There are no human rights without sovereignty. Instead of human rights being superior to sovereignty, human rights rely on sovereignty for protection. The formulation that 'human rights are superior to sovereignty' is not only absurd but detrimental to the cause of peace and development."[39]

However, with Saudi Arabia as with other states in the region, China has also attempted to downplay overt competition with the United States. During King Abdallah's "three firsts" visit, for example, Beijing reportedly reassured the United States that China was not attempting to create an alliance with Saudi Arabia against U.S. vital interests in the Middle East.[40] No communiqué or joint statement was issued in association with King Abdallah's visit. The official Chinese news agency Xinhua reported that President Hu Jintao and King Abdallah had agreed to "strengthen *pragmatic* cooperation and promote in-depth development of their strategic ties of friendship and cooperation" (emphasis added). This formulation used the key word "strategic" but was a bit less pointed than the push for "strategic cooperation" proclaimed in the more formal 1998 joint communiqué issued at the end of then–crown prince Abdallah's visit to China. The increased political content of Sino-Saudi relations and new tensions in Saudi-U.S. relations in 2006 made impolitic reference to "strategic cooperation."

The example of Saudi Arabia shows that China may develop and use its relationships with various Middle Eastern regimes to help nullify what it views as U.S. hegemonic aspirations. These actions must be taken, however, with subtlety sufficient to prevent damage to broader U.S.-China relations.

AGREEMENT AND DISAGREEMENT OVER IRAN

Iran provides a number of examples of Chinese avoidance of confrontation with the United States. It also demonstrates that Chinese cooperation cannot be taken for granted. China has long recognized Iran as major regional power. There is a tradition of strategic cooperation between the two countries going back to ancient times, which, after a period of disruption during the first two decades of the U.S. alliance with Iran under Mohammad Reza Shah Pahlavi and Chinese revolutionary activism under Mao Zedong, resumed in the early 1970s.

Beijing's preferred arrangement in the Persian Gulf—its alternative to domination by superpower hegemony there—was first laid out by Foreign Minister Ji Pengfei in 1973 during a visit to Iran, then still ruled by the Shah. Ji expressed the view that the security affairs of the

Persian Gulf region should be handled by the countries littoral to that body of water, not by extra-regional great powers. In 1973 this littoral principle represented an endorsement of Iran's drive for regional primacy, a drive also supported at the time by the United States. The Shah was deposed in 1979, and as relations between China and the Islamic Republic of Iran warmed in the mid-1980s, Beijing reiterated its support for the principle.[41] President Jiang Zemin again did so during his 2002 visit to Tehran.

In Iran, more than anywhere else in the Middle East, China has moved into the economic vacuum created by U.S. policy. Long-standing U.S. sanctions on Iran, combined with secondary sanctions intended to inhibit investment in the Iranian oil sector and (increasingly) dealings with Iranian financial entities, means Chinese companies face far less competition in Iranian markets than they do elsewhere. China first discovered rich Middle East commercial opportunities by supplying arms to both Iran and Iraq during their 1980–1988 war, ignoring a U.S. plan to cut off arms to Tehran. Iran's ambitious post-war development efforts, combined with Western reluctance, have created for China large markets in Iran for Chinese machinery, equipment, and engineering services—for which China received Iranian minerals and, especially, oil.

But China sometimes modified cooperation with Iran in order to reduce conflict with the United States. During the 1980s, China began supplying anti-ship missiles to Iran as part of Beijing's munitions supply relationship with Tehran during the Iran-Iraq War. As the "tanker war" escalated during the last years of that conflict, Washington became increasingly concerned that Iran would use Chinese-supplied missiles to attack lumbering oil tankers transiting the Persian Gulf and demanded that China stop supplying the missiles. After resisting U.S. demands for more than a year, Beijing finally agreed in March 1988 to end the anti-ship missile sales.[42] At the same time, China quietly provided Iran with machinery and equipment permitting Iran to indigenously manufacture more advanced anti-ship missiles.

It took much longer for Washington to secure Beijing's disengagement from nuclear, cruise missile, and category I (nuclear-capable) ballistic missile cooperation with Tehran. When Sino-Iranian cooperation in all these areas began in the mid-1980s, China was both an outsider in relation to the international nuclear nonproliferation regime and a major supplier of munitions to Iran. By the mid-1990s, there was robust cooperation between China and Iran in all three areas—cooperation paralleling and linked to the growing oil supply relationship between the two countries.

Objecting to Sino-Iranian nuclear and missile cooperation, Washington imposed 12 sets of sanctions on Chinese companies between 1987 and 2004 for selling banned items to Iran. In China's view, these were sanctions imposed on the basis of U.S. law, not by any international agreement to which China had acceded. China's support for Iranian missile and nuclear programs became a significant source of conflict in U.S.-China relations during the 1990s.

While resisting U.S. pressure to reduce cooperation with Iran, China also declined invitations from Iran to work together to play a more prominent role in checking the United States in the Middle East. With U.S.-China relations deteriorating after 1989 and China's anti-U.S. hegemony rhetoric at an all-time high, some leaders in Tehran decided that China and Iran should make a combined effort to push the United States from East Asia and the Persian Gulf respectively and broached this idea during various high-level exchanges. Beijing gently indicated disinterest in this proposal. Tehran also urged China to use its Security Council position to more forcefully support the Palestinians against Israel—even to the extent of seeking Israel's expulsion from the United Nations. China declined and in 1992 officially recognized Israel.

Constructive bargaining on the nuclear and missile issues began during the negotiations over the terms of the twinned U.S.-China presidential visits of 1997 and 1998, as part of the effort by Washington and Beijing to shift relations away from the confrontational track they had been on since 1989 and onto a more cooperative track. By early 1997, the two sides had agreed on a visit to the United States by President Jiang Zemin as part of the effort to "renormalize" U.S.-China relations. (Jiang's visit would be the first by a top Chinese leader to America since before the Beijing massacre.) Negotiations over the terms of that visit were intense. Beijing insisted on a formal state visit, with Jiang being accorded honors comparable to those provided to Deng Xiaoping on his 1979 visit—status that touched on Jiang's domestic legitimacy, establishing him in the linage of Mao Zedong and Deng Xiaoping. The U.S. side was willing to accept Beijing's requirements, but remained concerned over Chinese assistance to Iran's nuclear and missile program. Eventually, the two sides reached agreement. China ended *all* Chinese nuclear cooperation and Category I ballistic missile and advanced cruise missile cooperation, and Jiang Zemin got a high-profile state visit.[43]

It would be wrong though to conclude that Beijing rolled back its cooperation with Iran *because* Washington was willing to accord Jiang a formal state visit. Chinese leaders had probably decided to disengage from nuclear and missile cooperation with Iran in order to protect Sino-American amity, but decided to get whatever was possible from Washington in exchange for that move. For its part, the U.S. side handled this bargaining adroitly, going some distance to avoid embarrassing Beijing.

In the case of nuclear cooperation, China's acceptance of U.S. demands in 1997 went beyond the requirements of the Non-Proliferation Treaty (NPT), to which China had become a signatory in 1992. That treaty permits nuclear cooperation conducted under International Atomic Energy Agency (IAEA) supervision. China, however, agreed to suspend all nuclear cooperation with Iran, even activities that might be permitted under the NPT. CIA reports to Congress since 2001 on nonproliferation suggests that there may be some leakage in these agreements. Be that as it may, 1997 does seem to mark at least a very major curtailment of Sino-Iranian nuclear and missile cooperation. After 1997, U.S. objections to Sino-Iranian cooperation focused not on missiles, but on *dual-use* technologies and materials with potential missile production or chemical and biological warfare applications.

China began pressing in 1995 for a role in Iranian oil development. Those efforts finally paid off in October 2004 when a memorandum of understanding was signed giving Sinopec the lead in developing the new Yadavaran field in southwest Iran, straddling the border with Iraq and estimated to contain reserves of 3 billion barrels. Sinopec gained these development rights in exchange for an agreement to purchase, at market rates, 10 million tons of liquefied natural gas per year for 25 years. China thereby won its first major role in the development of Iranian oil, while Tehran secured a stable, long-term customer for Iran's natural gas. The total deal was estimated to be worth $100 billion. Some have argued that the Yadavaran deal was in part a reward to China for Beijing's support for Iran's struggles over its nuclear programs. It is more likely, however, that Iran had fewer other interested investors, in what was essentially a commercial transaction.

However, years of negotiation then followed the October 2004 award to Sinopec. Finally, in December 2007 Sinopec and the National Iranian Oil Company signed a $2 billion contract for the first-stage development of the Yadavaran field.[44] The reasons for the delay were in part political. The release in December 2007 of a U.S. National Intelligence

Estimate, stating that Iran had abandoned nuclear weapons development efforts in 2003, finally provided political cover for the deal to
move forward. Beyond the political issue, the Iranians are known to
be hard bargainers, especially in energy negotiations. It is also possible
then that the ongoing negotiations over various details took several
years to work out.

As the confrontation with Iran over its nuclear program started to
intensify in 2004, Washington began exerting strong pressure on Beijing to forgo cooperation with Iran on the development of Yadavaran.
As Jeff Bader, head of the Brookings Institution's China Initiative and a
onetime National Security Council China staffer under President Bill
Clinton, put it, the Iranian nuclear issue

> is an international community issue where it's important for China
> to step up to the plate and demonstrate its interest in stability in the
> region by looking very carefully at investments of this kind [Yada-
> varan] that might strengthen the Iranian regime and give Iran an op-
> tion to evade the Security Council and IAEA's [International Atomic
> Energy Agency] efforts to prevent them from going nuclear.[45]

In September 2005, Deputy Secretary of State Robert Zoellick called
on China to become a "responsible stakeholder" in dealing with major
international issues, including the Iran nuclear issue. "China's actions
on Iran's nuclear programs will reveal the seriousness of China's com-
mitments to nonproliferation," Zoellick said.[46] This was a U.S. call for
expanded U.S.-China cooperation and was seen as such by Beijing.
Dealing with the Iran nuclear issue was one area in which Washington
sought expanded Chinese cooperation. According to Iran's ambassador to China, Washington pressed Beijing to suspend oil and gas development cooperation with Iran.[47]

When Secretary of State Condoleezza Rice met in Egypt with Foreign Minister Yang Jiechi of China during the two-day conference on
Iraq in May 2007, she called for increased Chinese cooperation on Middle Eastern issues. Yang replied that "as a stakeholder and a constructive partner," China was willing to expand cooperation with the United
States.[48] The next month, when Rice met Vice Foreign Minister Dai
Bingguo in Washington for the fourth U.S.-China strategic dialogue,
Iran's nuclear program was among the issues discussed. The two sides
reportedly agreed to increase coordination and cooperation on various
issues that were discussed.[49]

It is interesting to note that while cooperation between China and Iraq on oil industry development was moving ahead with the revival of the al-Ahdab deal, cooperation between China and Iran on Yadavaran was stymied for three years. What these two circumstances appeared to have in common was increased cooperation between China and the United States in the Persian Gulf, at least until Beijing felt political circumstances would no longer mean that movement on Yadavaran would rouse U.S. ire.

To argue that China has repeatedly shown restraint so as to avoid confrontation with the United States in the Middle East is not to argue that China has not sometimes rejected U.S. demands. There appear to be three major instances of Chinese defiance of the United States on policy on the Middle East. All three involve Iran:

- The provision of Chinese munitions to Iran during the Iran-Iraq War of 1980–1988 in defiance of "Operation Staunch," a U.S. plan to force Tehran to a compromise peace by cutting off arms to Iran;

- Continued Chinese sales to Iran of technologies and materials with possible dual uses in chemical warfare or missile production, even after China's 1997 agreement with the United States to curtail nuclear and missile cooperation with Iran; and

- Opposition to strong sanctions against Iran over its nuclear programs.

As one author to this study has argued elsewhere, China recognizes Iran as a durable and like-minded major regional power with which cooperation has and will serve China's interests in many areas.[50] For this reason, Beijing is especially loath to sacrifice Iran to Sino-U.S. cooperation. Beijing balances its interest in maintaining and deepening ties with Iran against its interest in maintaining Sino-American comity. The latter objective does not always prevail, but the big picture seems to show the predominance of China's desire to minimize conflict with the United States. It is also possible that Washington has not been willing to pay the price demanded by Beijing for fuller satisfaction of U.S. demands regarding Iran. Beijing has bargained hard, typically expects a quid pro quo, and sometimes has obtained concessions in exchange for Chinese acquiescence to U.S. moves in the Middle East.

CHINA AND THE FUTURE OF IRAN'S NUCLEAR PROGRAMS

China's recent reactions to mounting U.S.-led international pressure on Iran to curb its nuclear programs offers an excellent example of Beijing's attempt to balance between cooperation with the United States on Middle Eastern issues and cultivation of cooperative relations with Middle Eastern countries—especially bigger, more powerful, oil-rich states such as Iran.

Even apart from proliferation concerns, the stakes on this issue are high—for China as for the rest of the world. A U.S.-Iran conflict—which many Chinese analysts believe is likely—would have an even greater impact on China's access to Middle Eastern oil than the Iraq War did. In 2006, for instance, Iran was China's third-largest foreign supplier of oil, after Angola and Saudi Arabia.[51] Most of Saudi and Iranian oil is shipped through Persian Gulf sea-lanes. Iran has long pledged that it would meet any Western attempt to restrict its oil exports with closure of these sea-lanes to the oil exports of other Gulf producers.

In 2005, the International Atomic Energy Agency determined that over a period of 18 years Iran had conducted a series of nuclear activities without reporting them to the IAEA as required under the NPT. This led to U.S. pressure to have the IAEA "refer" the Iran nuclear issue to the UN Security Council and to implementation of sanctions by the Security Council under Article 7 of the UN Charter dealing with "threats to peace."

China delayed, deflected, and softened U.S. efforts against Iran, while not actually blocking those efforts. The IAEA was the appropriate venue for dealing with the issue, Beijing insisted for nearly a year, thus opposing referral of the issue to the Security Council. China also repeatedly declared its support for Iran's "right to the peaceful use of nuclear energy" under the NPT and under IAEA inspection, implicitly rejecting the U.S. position (until 2007) that Iran's record of secret nuclear activities rendered it ineligible for virtually all such activities.

At the same time, Beijing found ways to cooperate with Washington (including by postponing implementation of the Yadavaran agreement). In January 2006, China sent a note to Iran parallel to notes from other members of the Permanent Five, warning it not to resume uranium enrichment. Beijing rejected a U.S. plan that a common note be issued jointly by the Permanent Five. Still, the note from Beijing went out.[52] Iranian intransigence and mounting pressure from the United

States and its allies caused Beijing to shift its position in March, when the Chinese representative on the IAEA Board of Governors (which operates by consensus) assented to a "report" on the Iran nuclear issue to the Security Council. "Referral" was changed to "report" at Beijing and Moscow's insistence, "referral" being used by the UN Charter to deal with the Security Council's treatment of "threats to international peace and security."

In July 2006, the Security Council approved Resolution 1696, which included a demand that Tehran suspend uranium enrichment. China, along with Russia, initially opposed any reference to Article 7 in the text of the resolution, out of concern that this would lead to sanctions that would further increase tensions. "The Chinese side feels that there has already been enough turmoil in the Middle East. We don't need any more turmoil," China's UN representative said.[53] At Beijing and Moscow's insistence, a U.S. proposal that the resolution declare Iran's nuclear programs a "threat to international peace and security" was deleted. But Resolution 1696 still invoked "Article 40 of Chapter 7" of the UN Charter authorizing "provisional measures" antecedent to the sanctions or use of force to deal with "threats to the peace" and "demand[ed]" on behalf of the Security Council "that Iran shall suspend all enrichment-related and reprocessing activities, including research and development, to be verified by the IAEA," and do so within 30 days.[54] Beijing and Moscow had secured extension of that deadline from the 14 days proposed by the United States.[55]

In high-level exchanges during 2006, Beijing repeatedly urged Tehran to respond "positively" and "flexibly" to various proposals put forward by the European Union or Russia. Iran should address the "legitimate concerns" of the "international community" over the possibly military nature of Iran's nuclear programs, China said. During Iranian president Mahmud Ahmadinejad's June visit to Beijing, for example, President Hu Jintao urged Iran to "earnestly study and actively respond to" a package of incentives agreed to a week previously by the EU-3 (Britain, France, and Germany), China, Russia, and the United States. "Positive feedback" on the plan could create an "important foundation" for peaceful resolution of the Iran nuclear issue, Hu said.[56]

When Tehran explicitly declared only days after the issuing of Resolution 1696 that it would continue uranium enrichment and ignore the August 31 deadline specified in the resolution, China joined with the other Permanent Five members and Germany in agreeing to begin implementing a series of graduated sanctions against Iran.[57] This laid the basis for China's assent to another sanctions measure, Resolution 1737, in December. The sanctions it called for were modest, with the only mandatory action being the freezing of funds of certain entities and the denial of travel rights to certain listed individuals. As was the case with Resolution 1696, in the negotiations for Resolution 1737 China worked to limit and water down sanctions. Still, China had agreed to sanctions against Iran, and also to the general principle of further sanctions if Iran did not come to terms with the IAEA.

In its handling of the Iranian nuclear issue, Beijing sought to prevent the United States from using the United Nations to implement strong economic sanctions or to justify military action against Iran. Beijing felt that such moves were inimical to China's efforts to expand economic cooperation, including efforts to ensure an uninterrupted oil supply, and would worsen tensions, making settlement of the issue more difficult and increasing the risk of war. The best way to thwart U.S. schemes, Beijing urged Tehran, was to maneuver diplomatically to win over moderate elements in Europe and Russia and thus isolate U.S. hard-liners favoring sanctions or military force. Iranian diplomatic inflexibility would only play into U.S. hands, Chinese representatives must have told their Iranian counterparts. Yet Beijing's bottom line was that Tehran should convince the international community—that is, not just the United States—that Iran's nuclear programs were not aimed at producing nuclear weapons. Within that framework, Iran's "legitimate right" to peaceful use of nuclear energy could be upheld. While China's methods differed from those of the United States, its ultimate objective was the same.

Most Chinese analysts we spoke with in early 2007 believed that Iran's nuclear programs were aimed at the development of nuclear weapons, not merely the use of nuclear power to generate electricity, as Tehran has claimed. Several analysts said that such a judgment lay behind China's 1997 agreement with the United States to disengage from all nuclear cooperation with Iran. No one we spoke with in Beijing asserted that Iran's programs were aimed only at civilian use, although several analysts claimed that the evidence of nuclear weapons objectives was inadequate.

All analysts we interviewed also expressed the belief that Iranian acquisition of nuclear weapons would be contrary to China's interests. Iranian nuclear weapons would lead to an escalation of tensions between countries in the region and probably to a chain reaction of region-wide proliferation of nuclear weapons, these analysts said. China would then be almost completely surrounded by nuclear weapon states. China's status as one of only a few nuclear powers would be diluted. Iran might use its weapons against Israel or to support a push for greater influence in the Persian Gulf region. Iranian nuclear weapons might make their way into terrorist hands; regardless of whom those weapons were then used against—the United States or China—this would not be in China's interests. In numerous ways, Iranian nuclear weapons would be antithetical to conditions of low tension, open borders, and stability, all of which are good for Chinese business and thus the success of China's development drive. No Chinese analyst intimated that Iranian possession of nuclear weapons might help check U.S. hegemony in the Persian Gulf and elsewhere in the world. When asked explicitly about this possibility, all directly, and sometimes heatedly, denied it (along, of course, with the implication that China might favor Iranian possession of nuclear weapons).

But the Chinese also believe that U.S. policy bears much responsibility for whatever Iranian determination exists to develop nuclear weapons. There is a long litany of U.S. moves putatively responsible for this desire on Iran's part: a refusal to establish diplomatic relations with the Islamic Republic of Iran, sanctions, military strikes against Iran during the Iran-Iraq War, the labeling of Iran as part of an "axis of evil," talk of "regime change" by high U.S. officials, and U.S. military deployments to the Persian Gulf—including the 2006 deployment of an additional aircraft carrier and Patriot missile batteries. These U.S. policies of threat and pressure vindicate any Iranian desire to build nuclear weapons, even if they are not its cause. The best way to dissuade Tehran from seeking nuclear weapons would be to end threats to Iran's security, Chinese analysts believe.

Chinese analysts also point out that Iran sees itself as a major power and great civilization and is determined to secure the appropriate respect from the rest of the world, starting with the United States. The United States should recognize this Iranian craving for respect, Chinese analysts recommend. Instead of treating Iran like a rogue state, the United States should shift course and seek rapprochement, offering not only respect but formal diplomatic recognition, economic ties, and security in exchange for abandonment of any aspiration to possess nuclear weapons. One analyst suggested that the United States treat

Iran the same way the Nixon administration treated China in 1971—as a respected big power with legitimate national interests—and on this basis work out an understanding with the Islamic Republic.

The Chinese believe that Beijing has played a significant and positive role in nudging Iran toward acceptance of global nonproliferation norms. Having disengaged from nuclear cooperation with Iran in 1997, Beijing has consistently called on Tehran to fulfill all its obligations under the NPT, which is a diplomatic way of calling for Iran to abandon any quest for nuclear weapons. In the maneuvering at the IAEA during 2004–2005, China urged Tehran to accept an Additional Protocol subjecting Iran's nuclear program to more stringent inspections (which Iran under President Mohammad Khatami agreed to do); to continue implementation of that protocol; to suspend and then resume suspension of uranium enrichment; and to address the "reasonable concerns" of the international community regarding possible Iranian development of nuclear weapons. Both before and after China voted "yes" on Security Council Resolution 1696 in July 2006 and Resolution 1737 in December 2006 (both of which moved toward weak sanctions against Iran), China had long, detailed, and sincere talks with Iran in an attempt to persuade it to make the necessary compromises. In these talks, China told Iran that nuclear weapons would not increase Iran's security, but would lead instead to greater international isolation, pressure, and regional proliferation. Chinese representatives also warned Tehran that conflict with the United States was a real possibility that Iran needed to avoid. (This echoed China's advice to Tehran during the tanker war of 1986–1987 and to Baghdad prior to the 2003 war.)

China's advice probably carries weight in Iran. Since the middle period of the Iran-Iraq War, Beijing has been an important supporter and adviser of Tehran. Comments by Iranian leaders over the years indicate that China is regarded as Iran's trusted friend. China is also one of only a few countries in a position to assist Iran. The contrasting situation of Russia is instructive in this regard. As a member of the Permanent Five, Russia has a veto in the Security Council. Also, Russia can supply Iran with advanced technology. But Russia's economy is far less dynamic than China's, and Russia has far less influence globally than China. Nor is Russia, unlike China, a civilizational comrade of Iran. Russia, unlike China, was Iran's historical nemesis. When arguments that nuclear weapons would diminish rather than enhance Iranian security are made by Americans, Europeans, or Russians, those arguments probably seem self-serving to Iranians. When they come from Chinese, they are probably more persuasive.

According to a former Chinese ambassador to Iran, China's endorsement of weak sanctions against Iran in 2006 was intended to send the message to Tehran that the international community was united, and that Tehran would not be able to play one power against another. Tehran had entertained illusions that China would not join the United States and Europe in punishing Iran for its continued enrichment and reprocessing of uranium. China's endorsement of weak sanctions indicated that this was wrong, the former ambassador said.

In terms of an ultimate solution, China is willing to accept Iranian civilian nuclear programs. This is in contrast to China's stance toward North Korea, which Beijing believes should completely suspend all nuclear programs. The reason for this, an analyst explained, is that in Iran, unlike North Korea, China has no "strategic interests." China's interests in the Middle East are mainly economic, while in North Korea the Chinese have significant political and security interests.

So, in the absence of perceived strategic interests, what quid pro quo could the United States offer to China to gain its active and significant support for a nuclear-free Iran? (This time a state visit will not be enough.) Perhaps one place to start would be to offer a further expanded economic role for China in Iraq, building on last year's al-Ahdab agreement. The United States could also offer to bless (or even actively support) the further development of the Sino-Saudi economic partnership. Those elements, taken along with the continued desire by Beijing to maintain good relations with Washington, might be enough to bring China along. Such an approach could also help shift China's more general Middle East calculus, improving the prospects for cooperation across the region.

THE TAIWAN FACTOR

Taiwan is a major factor in China's foreign policy calculations that enters in two main ways into the equation of U.S.-PRC cooperation or rivalry in the Middle East.

- Beijing attempts to use U.S. demands for Chinese cooperation in the Middle East as leverage to secure U.S. concessions on Taiwan.

- Beijing's calculations regarding a possible war with the United States over Taiwan increases the importance of having powerful and independent-minded oil-producing friends in the Middle East that will be willing to supply oil in such a contingency.

Regarding the first factor, clearly Beijing has tried to establish such a linkage. During the 1997 negotiations over termination of Chinese nuclear and missile cooperation with Iran, Beijing pressed for a written, public commitment, preferably in a joint communiqué issued at the forthcoming Jiang-Bush summit, affirming pledges made by Clinton in a private mid-1995 letter to Jiang: the United States would not support Taiwan independence, the creation of two Chinas, or Taiwan's admission to the United Nations. Washington refused. Beijing countered that this refusal would endanger the summit. Washington called Beijing's bluff, and Beijing executed a volte-face. At his joint press conference with Jiang during the summit, however, Clinton merely gave verbal reiterations of past U.S. agreements with Beijing about Taiwan.[58] Several years later during the August 2002 visit to Beijing, when he delivered the U.S. concession on ETIM that was discussed earlier, Armitage reiterated that the United States does not support Taiwan independence.[59] It may be that Armitage was again responding to Chinese demands for concessions on Taiwan by reiterating earlier U.S. positions on Taiwan. Later during the intense U.S.-PRC talks over Iraq in February 2003, an "adviser" to the Chinese government said that a key point in the successful outcome of those negotiations would be whether Washington was willing to show greater "flexibility" on the Taiwan issue. "We are not linking the issues," the man said. "But what we are saying is this: The United States cannot expect us to continually give unless it gives something too. That's how the real world works."[60]

Regarding the second factor (the role of Middle East states in the event of a U.S.-PRC war over Taiwan), both Beijing and Washington would initially attempt to keep such a war limited in duration and geographic scope. But either government might also decide that protraction and geographic expansion were preferable to accepting defeat (which would probably mean the loss of Taiwan). In the event of a protracted war, Washington's advantage would be its naval supremacy and the consequent ability to deny China any or all seaborne imports. Oil would probably be a prime U.S. target.

This is one reason why China is building overland oil pipelines into China. Neutral states have often been willing to serve as transport corridors for states at war, and Middle East oil might reach China by pipeline via, say, Myanmar or Kazakhstan. But China would also need friendly governments in major oil-producing countries willing and able to resist U.S. pressure and continue supplying China with oil by whatever means could be arranged. Iran is the major oil-producing state most likely to cooperate with such arrangements, and this is one reason why Beijing is so reluctant to alienate Tehran by siding more fully with the United States. Strategic understanding with Iran is a hedge against the extreme contingency of U.S. blockade or embargo.

The United States has insisted that Taiwan and Middle East issues cannot be linked. Yet if Beijing insists on linking Taiwan to U.S.-PRC discussions of Middle East issues and resists U.S. demands for greater cooperation absent comparable U.S. "cooperation" on Taiwan issues, U.S. negotiators may find it difficult to resist Beijing's demands. On the other hand, Chinese insistence on such linkage may be short-sighted. It fosters in the United States the perception that China is a rival in the Middle East and that China will someday use its power to attack Taiwan. If China came to be perceived in the United States as a partner in the Middle East, those positive perceptions would almost certainly influence U.S. handling of the Taiwan issue in ways favorable to Beijing.

Efforts to reduce tensions over Taiwan—in ways that do not damage the U.S. interest in the continuing peaceful lives of the people of Taiwan—should have positive effects on U.S.-PRC cooperation in the Middle East. As the prospect for a U.S.-PRC war over Taiwan diminishes, so too will the incentive to cultivate Iran as a hedge against that increasingly remote contingency.

Notes

1. Shu Zhang, "Several Questions Calling for Deep Thought," *Shijie Zhishi*, March 1, 1991, 1.

2. Li Qingong, "Special Article: Bush's State of the Union Address and the New U.S. Global Strategy," *Shijie Zhishi*, March 1, 1991, 5.

3. "Fiendish Plot," *Far Eastern Economic Review* 151, issue 5 (January 31, 1991): 6.

4. "HK Paper: China's Official Media Breaks Silence, Attacks U.S. War on Iraq," *The Standard* (Hong Kong), February 19, 2003.

5. "Security or Hegemony," *Beijing Review*, April 10, 2003, 43.

6. "Li Guofu Predicts Iran Will Be Next U.S. Target," *Wen Hui Po* (Hong Kong), March 21, 2003.

7. Zhou Yihuang, "U.S. Attack on Iraq: Killing Three Birds with One Stone," *Jiefangjun Bao*, September 16, 2002.

8. Agence France Presse, BBC Monitoring, March 4, 2004.

9. "Quotes from China," BBC Monitoring, March 4, 2004.

10. Wang Changyi, "Middle East Initiative Queried," *Beijing Review*, April 1, 2004, 12–13.

11. Reuters, "War Destroyed Global Anti-Terror Coalition: China," November 2, 2004.

12. National Bureau of Statistics of China, *China Statistical Yearbook 2005* (Beijing: China Statistics Press, 2005), 740–741.

13. Qian Qichen, *Waijiao Shi Ji* (Ten diplomatic episodes) (Beijing: *Shijie Zhish chubanshei*, 2003), 72–101, 98–99, 184–188.

14. Waiel Faleh, "Saddam Condemns UN Security Council Members for Inaction," Associated Press, December 23, 2000, http://www.globalpolicy.org/security/sanction/iraq1/civflight/001223.htm; "Several Airlines Propose to resume Flights to Iraq," Reuters, December 17, 2000, http://www.globalpolicy.org/security/sanction/iraq1/civflight/001217.htm.

15. Bill Gertz, "China Fortifying Iraq's Air-Defense System," *Washington Times*, February 20, 2001; "China Reassures Powell on Iraq Dealings," *New York Times*, March 9, 2001, http://query.nytimes.com/gst/fullpage.html?res=9A0DE4DC173AF93AA35750C0A9679C8B63.

16. William Safire, "The CIA's China Tilt," *New York Times*, July 9, 2001, http://query.nytimes.com/gst/fullpage.html?res=9905E4DB1038F93AA35754C0A9679C8B63.

17. Eric Eckholm, "In Shift, China Seems to Back a Resolution on Iraq," *New York Times*, September 26, 2002, http://query.nytimes.com/gst/fullpage.html?res=990CE7D91039F935A1575AC0A9649C8B63.

18. "Senior Official Calls Bush-Jiang Meeting 'Very Positive,'" GlobalSecurity.org, October 26, 2002, http://www.globalsecurity.org/wmd/library/news/china/2002/prc-021026-usia01.htm.

19. "Joint Statement by China, France, and Russia Interpreting UN Security Council Resolution 1441," November 8, 2002, http://www.staff.city.ac.uk/p.willetts/IRAQ/FRRSCHST.HTM.

20. "Iraq Declaration: Russia-France-Germany," French Mission to the United Nations, March 5, 2003.

21. "HK Journal Views China's Iraq Position, Suggests Seeking U.S. Concessions in Return for Support," *Hsin Pao*, February 18, 2003.

22. John Pomfret, "China Offers Help—With Conditions," *Washington Post*, September 18, 2001; Erik Eckholm, "China's About-Face; Support for

U.S. on Terror," *New York Times*, September 30, 2001, http://query.nytimes .com/gst/fullpage.html?res=9A00E2D8173DF933A0575AC0A9679C8B63.

23. For the chronology of the U.S. movement toward the 2003 invasion of Iraq, see Bob Woodward, *Plan of Attack* (New York: Simon and Schuster, 2004).

24. "China-U.S. Secret Agreement on Iraq and North Korea," *Korea Web Weekly*, February 3, 2002, http://www.kimsoft.com/2003/US-China.htm.

25. "China's Envoy Defends UN Deal on Iraq," *Financial Times*, October 19, 2003.

26. "Iraq Revives Oil Deal with China, " *Al Alam News*, June 24, 2007, http://www.iraqdirectory.com/DisplayNews.aspx?id=4001; David Winning, "Iraq Woos China to Revive Neglected Oil Industry," *Dow Jones International News*, October 28, 2006, http://www.uofaweb.ualberta.ca/chinainstitute/ nav03.cfm?nav03=52106&nav02=43875&nav01=43092.

27. Yitzhak Shichor, "East Wind over Arabia: Origins and Implications of the Sino-Saudi Missile Deal," *The China Quarterly*, no. 126 (June 1991): 60–61.

28. Nuclear Threat Initiative, "China's Missile Exports and Assistance to Saudi Arabia," 2007, http://www.nti.org/db/china/msarpos.htm.

29. Steven R. McDowell, "Is Saudi Arabia a Nuclear Threat?" Naval Post Graduate School, September 2003, http://www.fas.org/irp/threat/mcdowell .pdf.

30. "King of Saudi Arabia Ends China Visit," *Zhongguo tongxun she*, January 26, 2006.

31. "China's Hainan Kicks off Oil Storage Project," *Platts Oilgram News* 85, no. 247 (December 14, 2007): 3; "HK Paper: China, Saudi Arabia to Jointly Build Hainan Oil Reserve Base," *Wen Wei Po*, January 24, 2006.

32. Khaled Almaeena, "Kingdom, China Sign Landmark Energy Pact," *Arab News*, January 24, 2006, http://www.arabnews.com/?page=1&section =0&article=76724&d=24&m=1&y=2006.

33. Xinhua, "Saudi Crown Prince Meets PRC Deputy Foreign Minister Yang Wenchang," October 27, 2002.

34. Ibid.

35. Xinhua, "Chinese FM Li Zhaoxing Consults over Telephone with His Saudi Arabian Counterpart," May 12, 2003.

36. Ahmad Majed Al Aitan, "Washington's Greater Middle East Initiative: A Regional Perspective," NATO Defense College, 2005, http://www.ndc.nato .int/download/publications/al_aitan.pdf.

37. "ZTS Roundup: 'Sino-Saudi Summit Achieves Success,'" *Zhongguo Tongxunshe*, April 24, 2006.

38. Xinhua, "Report by Reporters Kong Yan, Luo Hui, Hu Jintao holds talks with Saudi King Abdullah," January 24, 2006.

39. "Editorial Lauds Jiang's Six-Nation Tour," *Ta Kong Pao*, November 5, 1999.

40. Eric Teo Chu Cheow, "China's Emerging Role in the Middle East," *PacNet*, February 23, 2006, http://www.csis.org/media/csis/pubs/pac0607 .pdf.

41. Beijing paired the littoral principle in 1984 with endorsement of a U.S.-backed UN Security Council resolution condemning attacks on neutral shipping in the Persian Gulf—attacks conducted mostly by Iran.

42. John Garver, *China and Iran: Ancient Partners in a Post-Imperial World* (Seattle: University of Washington Press, 2006), 205–208.

43. Ibid., 224–228.

44. "Iran signals Sanctions Alert by $2bn Oil Deal with China group," *Financial Times*, December 10, 2007, http://www.ft.com/cms/s/0/e020dcb6 -a6c3-11dc-b1f5-0000779fd2ac.html.

45. Luis Ramirez, "China-Iran Posed to Proceed on Oil Deal despite the Nuclear Impasse," Voice of America, February 23, 2006, http://www.voanews .com/english/archive/2006-02/2006-02-23-voa29.cfm.

46. Robert B. Zoellick, "Whither China: From Membership to Responsibility?" Remarks to National Committee on U.S.-China Relations, September 21, 2005, http://www.ncuscr.org/articlesandspeeches/Zoellick.htm.

47. "HK: Iranian Ambassador to PRC 'Confident' on Sino-Iranian Energy Cooperation," *Ming Bao*, January 27, 2007.

48. Xinhua, "Xinhua: PRC FM Meets Rice in Egypt," May 4, 2007.

49. Xinhua, "PRC Vice FM Dai Binguo Meets US Secretary of State," June 23, 2007.

50. Garver, *China and Iran*.

51. Energy Information Agency, "China's Crude Oil Imports by Source (Thousand bbl/d)."

52. Elaine Sciolino, "Iran, Defiant, Insists It Plans to Restart Nuclear Program," *New York Times*, January 10, 2006, http://www.nytimes.com/2006/01/10/ international/middleeast/10iran.html.

53. Joel Brinkley, "Rice Floats the Idea of UN Sanctions on Iran, but China and Russia Reject It," *New York Times*, March 31, 2006, http://www.nytimes .com/2006/03/31/world/31diplo.html?_r=1&oref=slogin.

54. UN Security Council, Department of Public Information, "Security Council Demands Iran Suspend Uranium Enrichment by 31 August, or Face Possible Economic, Diplomatic Sanctions," July 31, 2006, http://www.un.org/News/Press/docs/2006/sc8792.doc.htm.

55. Warren Hoge, "New UN Draft on Iran Softens Condemnation," *New York Times*, March 29, 2006, http://www.nytimes.com/2006/03/29/international/middleeast/29iran.html.

56. Chinese Ministry of Foreign Affairs, "MFA briefing," June 13, 2006, http://wwwfmprc.gov.cn.

57. Philip Shenon, "U.S. Cites Deal with U.N. Members to Punish Iran," *New York Times*, October 7, 2006, http://www.nytimes.com/2006/10/07/world/middleeast/07iran.html?ex=1317873600&en=fc10410fd2377961&ei=5088&partner=rssnyt&emc=rss.

58. James Mann, *About Face: A History of America's Curious Relation with China from Nixon to Clinton* (New York: Alfred Knopf, 1999), 134–135.

59. "Armitage Says U.S. Does Not Support Taiwan Independence," GlobalSecurity.org, August 26, 2002, http://www.globalsecurity.org/wmd/library/news/taiwan/2002/roc-020826-usia01.htm.

60. John Pomfret, "Beijing Is Cool to Powell's Pleas," *Washington Post*, February 25, 2003.

CHAPTER THREE

THE MIDDLE EAST

Many Middle Eastern states have had long and involved histories with the United States, but they see China as an investment in their future. Contemporary Middle Eastern views of China are similar to Middle Eastern views of the United States a century ago, when many in the Middle East looked to the United States to rescue them from European imperialism. Aloof from the struggles that had tested the Middle East throughout the nineteenth century and largely without clients in the region, an earlier generation of Middle Easterners saw the United States as precisely the kind of honest broker that could help forge states from the ashes of the Ottoman Empire. President Wilson's championing of the idea of self-determination had helped buff American credentials, and although there was disappointment in some quarters that the United States would not accept the Mandate for Palestine, the refusal served to reinforce the notion that, unlike European countries, the United States sought neither power nor subjects in the Middle East.

Contemporary Middle Eastern views of the United States tend to take the opposite view, seeing the United States inheriting the role of Imperial Britain and shaping its policies in such a way as to advance imperial power at the expense of subject peoples.

It was confidence in the sincerity of American anti-colonialism a century ago that paved the way for U.S. influence in the Middle East. The United States was in the practice of sending businessmen, not viceroys, and was welcomed in the region because of it. Lacking both scholarship and administrative experience in the Middle East—and with few Americans other than missionaries who had spent much time in the region at all—the United States won affection for exercising a light hand in Arab lands. One hears echoes of these views in early twenty-first century perceptions of China.

World War II changed the U.S. relationship with the Middle East fundamentally. The war transformed oil into a strategic global commodity and thrust the United States to the position of superpower. The superpower role was not self-evident, however. In the early days of the Cold War, the United States allied itself with progressive forces as it sought to stave off communist revolution in Egypt and elsewhere. U.S. efforts were directed not so much at securing ruling oligarchies as loosening the oligarchs' grip on the population. Land reform, land reclamation and vast irrigation projects—often carried out with surplus military equipment that the United States left in the region—were typical of the early approach that won goodwill for the United States. Within a few years, however, much had changed. The rise of nationalism and its concomitant quest for nonalignment in the Cold War helped push the U.S. government toward forging close alliances with conservative monarchies that shared Washington's antipathy to Moscow and pro-Soviet Arab regimes.

Anti-Americanism flared in the aftermath of the 1967 Arab-Israeli War, in which many thought the United States tilted unfairly toward Israel. Hostility also ran high after the U.S.-brokered 1978 peace negotiations between Egypt and Israel, which most Arabs saw as treasonous rather than triumphant. Still, fear of communism and the Soviet Union trumped Arab dissatisfaction with the American role. When the United States government sought Arab support for *mujahideen* fighting to repel the Soviet invasion of Afghanistan, billions flowed from Arab coffers, while some Middle East governments facilitated the movement of young men to Pakistan and Afghanistan to wage jihad against the Soviets and their Afghan Communist allies.

Throughout this period, China was a bit player in the minds of most Middle Eastern actors. Although China's leaders mouthed support for liberation movements around the world, material support was forthcoming only for the Palestine Liberation Organization in the mid-1960s and for the insurgency in southern Oman throughout the 1960s. The Soviet Union was the major anti-U.S. force in the Middle East[1] (especially in larger states such as Egypt, Iran, and Iraq), but China was not. The country was too consumed with internal challenges, and too concerned with checking Soviet ambitions closer to home, to play a significant role thousands of miles away.[2]

Middle Eastern states profited from the Cold War, even as their populations sometimes suffered. Their borders were largely stable, save for the 1967 Arab-Israeli War, and regimes successfully overcame most internal challenges. For those tied to Moscow, subsidies and scholarships helped modernize often primitive societies. For those allied with the West, investment poured into their coffers under the protective aegis of U.S. troops and support. The United States aided some and protected others; over time, more and more came under the U.S. sway. In time, with the collapse of the Soviet Union, the U.S. triumph was almost complete. By the end of the twentieth century, virtually all of the states in the Middle East had strong and positive relations with the United States. That number continued to grow after the turn of the century as Libya reversed its antagonistic relationship with the United States and U.S.-led forces deposed Saddam Hussein.

Although the end of the Cold War vindicated the judgment of many, it also helped undermine the logic of the region's pro-U.S. orientation. With less need for a defender, governments and their publics grew more critical of the U.S. relationship, and absent the Cold War, the United States downscaled many of its efforts in the region.

The events of September 11, 2001, were a tremendous jolt to how the United States and the Middle East saw each other. The attacks aroused tremendous sentiment in the United States in favor of transforming the Middle East and stemming what many Americans saw as the region's seething hatred. Close bilateral relationships between governments persisted, but those relationships became more complex and tense. Calls for energy independence rang out in the halls of Congress,[3] and some intellectuals began touting conservation more as a foreign policy imperative than as an environmental one. The prominent *New York Times* columnist Thomas Friedman wrote in 2006:

> We need a president and a Congress with the guts not just to invade Iraq, but to also impose a gasoline tax and inspire conservation at home. That takes a real energy policy with long-term incentives for renewable energy—wind, solar, biofuels—rather than the welfare-for-oil-companies-and-special-interests that masqueraded last year as an energy bill.[4]

Arabs responded to the new U.S. mood with feelings of resentment and betrayal. Former Saudi ambassador to the United States Prince Turki al-Faisal, for example, told a conference in February 2007, "It has become very fashionable for (U.S.) politicians to use the word 'energy independence' or 'independence from foreign oil,' and that is basically a political canard politicians and technocrats use."[5] In a 2006 *Al Jazeera* television debate, Eid bin Mas'oud al-Jahni, the director of the Gulf Center for Energy Research, said with disgust, "I think that the future of Gulf oil is in the Far East and in Europe."[6] Interestingly, while the U.S. calls for energy independence were dutifully translated in the Arabic press, most of the commentary it evinced was in English rather than Arabic. The silence was a sign of how deeply offended and threatened the attacks made many Arab leaders feel. It is into this growing breech that China has quietly stepped.

China cannot supplant the United States in the Middle East as a military power, lacking anything close to the requisite military might. Yet, Middle Eastern countries can use a relationship with China to supplement the bilateral relations with the United States and perhaps give those countries the freedom of greater distance from Washington. China is playing the game well. Unlike the Soviet Union, whose frequently heavy-handed reach in the Middle East prompted most countries to flee for the U.S. security umbrella, Middle Eastern states of all stripes welcome China. China's approach is the opposite of the old Soviet approach: Beijing entices with economics and flattery, and it studiously avoids confrontation with the United States over Middle East issues. The economic capabilities and the cultural appeal of China's ancient but rapidly and seemingly successfully modernizing society also far exceed those of the former Soviet Union. Middle Eastern states have been eager to develop commercial relationships with China given its demographic weight, surging economy, and political neutrality.

For Middle Eastern energy exporters, oil and gas form the crux of their relationship with China. Beyond energy, trade in manufacturing, capital flows, and arms sales have also boosted China–Middle East relationships. In return, the Middle East has imported low-cost consumer goods, machinery, equipment, and vehicles of all sorts from Chinese factories. Oil money from the Gulf has also flowed into China, and arms sales have remained important as well.

Political and security issues have also increasingly driven this relationship in recent years as tension in U.S.–Middle East ties has mounted.

China's international prominence has made it an attractive target for lobbying by Middle Eastern states, particularly on the Iranian nuclear issue and the Arab-Israeli peace process. China's hands-off policy on domestic political matters has also made it popular in comparison to the active U.S. stance, and China's cultural appeal has grown as well.

SAUDI ARABIA: THE PIVOTAL STATE

Of all the Arab states finding themselves between the United States and China, Saudi Arabia is the most pivotal among them, and of all of the Middle Eastern countries, Saudi Arabia has courted China most assiduously. As mentioned above, King Abdallah's first overseas trip upon ascending the throne was to China. His visit in January 2006 made him the first Saudi king ever to visit the People's Republic. In 2007, Saudi Arabia (along with Angola) was China's largest source of foreign oil, exporting more than a half million bbl/d. By the end of the decade, Saudi and Chinese officials expect that number to double.[7] Saudi exports to China have grown remarkably quickly; as recently as 1995, Saudi Arabia ranked twenty-fifth among China's suppliers.[8]

China is well positioned to build an energy partnership with Saudi Arabia. Relative to other energy producers, Saudi Arabia's energy development is well organized and well capitalized. It needs steady consumers rather than investment, and it is here that China provides a welcome alternative to the seemingly capricious consuming markets of the United States. Of the estimated 8.6 million bbl/d of petroleum liquids exported by Saudi Arabia, half of Saudi production currently goes to markets in Asia (including Japan, South Korea, China, and India), and that demand is growing (figure 3.1).[9] In 2007, China imported an average of 500,000 bbl/d from Saudi Arabia. By comparison, Japan, Saudi Arabia's largest customer, imported an estimated 1.5 million bbl/d.[10]

One of Saudi Arabia's most important needs is a market for its "distressed" medium-grade crude oil—a viscous, acidic, often sulfurous product that Saudi Arabia has in abundance but that has few takers on the international market. Also referred to as heavy crude, it sells at a 15 to 25 percent discount over premium grades of oil, but there are a limited number of refineries that can transform it into products such as heating oil and gasoline.[11] Building new refineries in the United States is virtually out of the question, because of a range of environmental

Figure 3.1. Saudi Exports by Region: Crude Oil

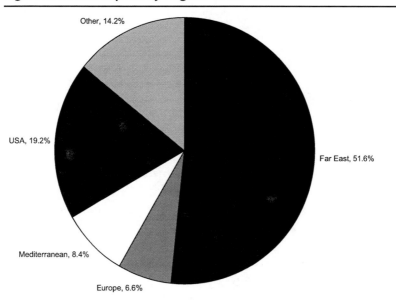

Source: Saudi Aramco, *Facts and Figures 2006,* 35, available at http://www.saudiaramco.com/irj/go/
km/docs/SaudiAramcoPublic/FactsAndFigures/F%26F2006/2006_FactsAndFigures_EN.pdf.

concerns. Heavy crude may constitute an increasing percentage of Saudi energy production in the future, particularly as its main fields grow old and as Aramco develops an offshore Gulf field in Manifa that aims to produce 900,000 bbl/d of heavy crude by 2011.

Saudi Arabia has been working to develop China's capacity to purchase and use Saudi heavy crude, investing in two refineries along China's coast. These investments include Saudi Aramco's pending purchase of a 25 percent stake in the Qingdao refinery in China's Shandong province, scheduled to refine 200,000 bbl/d by 2008.[12] Aramco will also be the primary long-term crude provider for the Quanzhou refinery in the Fujian province, scheduled to refine 240,000 bbl/d by early 2009. In addition Saudi Arabia is developing two new refinery projects in Saudi Arabia designed to handle the heavy crude for export, including 400,000 bbl/d facilities in Yanbu' on the Red Sea coast and Jubail on the Gulf coast that will receive crude oil from the Manifa offshore field beginning in 2011.[13] Both sides evince a keen desire to create a steady and reliable commercial relationship based on Saudi Arabia's export of heavy crude.

This is not to say that the Saudis have turned against the United States, which remains both the world's largest consumer of oil and the principal destination for Saudi students studying abroad. Over the last decade of U.S. crude oil imports, Saudi Arabia has consistently been among the top five sources and in 2007 ranked second after Canada.[14] Total U.S. gross imports were around 13 million bbl/d in 2007, and of that nearly 1.5 million bbl/d came from Saudi Arabia (figures 3.2 and 3.3).

The Saudi government is also investing in the U.S. bilateral relationship. It is putting millions of dollars into scholarships for students to study in the United States, and government-to-government cooperation on a range of security issues remains intimate. But the U.S. demand for oil is relatively flat, and politics continue to complicate bilateral relations. For all of the closeness of the Saudi-American relationship, Saudis clearly judge it as increasingly insufficient to meet Saudi security needs. There is a growing sense that U.S. policymakers are making critical mistakes across the region that ultimately threaten Saudi interests, most importantly in Iraq. For their part, Americans have never judged the relationship to be more than a single piece in a very large global puzzle.

SECURITY

Where the United States remains preeminent in Saudi minds is in the area of security. The U.S.-Saudi defense relationship dates to World War II and actually predates the large-scale production of oil in Saudi Arabia. Most of the smaller Gulf sheikhdoms had established defensive ties to the United Kingdom decades before the discovery of oil; the Al Saud on the Arabian peninsula were not only not part of the British domain, but they often threatened British power. It was the presence of UK defense relationships that helped protect sheikhdoms such as Bahrain, the Trucial States, and Transjordan in the 1920s from the advances of Saudi forces from the deserts of Najd in central Arabia, as the new kingdom of Saudi Arabia was defining its territorial scope. By the time they stopped, Saudi troops had brought Arabia's two greatest assets under Saudi control: the Muslim holy places of the Hijaz and what were swiftly discovered to be the oil-rich lands in the Eastern Province.

By the 1940s, the new Saudi state was potentially rich but in fact quite poor. With a huge strategic asset under its sands, it needed the

Figure 3.2. U.S. Oil Imports from Saudi Arabia

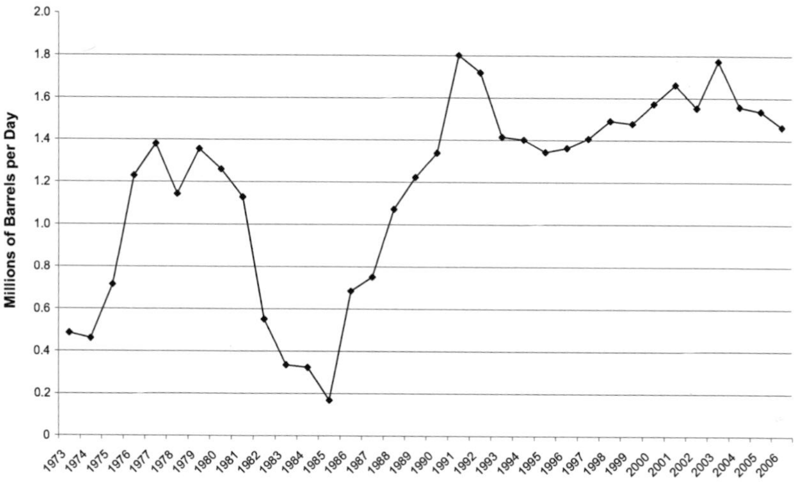

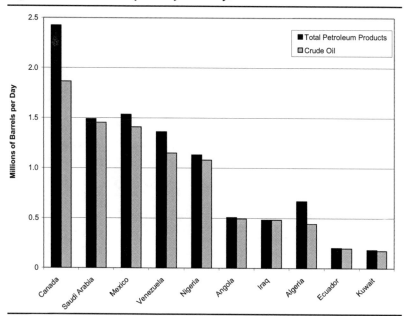

Source: U.S. Energy Information Administration, available at http://tonto.eia.doe.gov/dnav/pet/hist/mttimussa2a.htm.

Figure 3.3. U.S. Oil Imports by Country, 2007

Note: The data in the tables above exclude oil imports into the U.S. territories.

Source: U.S. Energy Information Administration, "Crude Oil and Total Petroleum Imports Top 15 Countries," March 3, 2008, available at http://www.eia.doe.gov/pub/oil_gas/petroleum/data_publications/company_level_imports/current/import.html.

protection of a great power it could trust. King Abdel Aziz ibn Saud chose the United States over the United Kingdom. President Franklin Roosevelt helped solidify that trust in 1943 when he extended Lend-Lease aid in exchange for permission to establish an airbase at Dhahran and met ibn Saud on the Bitter Lake on the Egyptian coast in 1945. Even so, the relationship was somewhat distant and relatively straightforward.

It was not until a quarter century later that the U.S.-Saudi relationship became strategically vital for both countries. The sharp rise in oil prices in the early 1970s made Saudi Arabia a spectacularly wealthy place and consequently a suddenly far more influential one. The country's effective use of "the oil weapon" after the 1973 Arab-Israeli War thrust it into the leadership of the Arab world, which was still searching for a leader after the demise of Egypt's Gamal Abdel Nasser. U.S. trade with Saudi Arabia skyrocketed, mostly on trade in oil: from $2.6 billion in 1974 to $8.6 billion in 1976 to $10.2 billion in 1978.[15] Equally important, Saudi decisions to pump or not to pump oil (in those days of plentiful excess capacity) had a material impact on the U.S. economy and thus on the political fortunes of U.S. politicians.

It was in this period that the U.S. military became intimately involved in supplying and training the swiftly growing Saudi military forces and also established an exceedingly close relationship with the National Guard, the tribal force close to the king. U.S. primacy in the region grew still further in the wake of the British pullout from the Gulf in 1971. The decades-long Saudi bet on the United States seemed vindicated.

But as the U.S.-Saudi relationship grew deeper, it also grew more complicated. King Faisal was a determined supporter of the Palestinian cause, and through the 1960s and 1970s the United States became a closer and closer ally of Israel. Differences over policy toward Israel (articulated in bitter Saudi opposition to the 1978 Camp David negotiations) helped highlight the stark differences between U.S. and Saudi society. Saudi Arabia in the 1970s was becoming a more cosmopolitan place, as earlier efforts to promote literacy, communication, and transportation in the desert kingdom had begun to yield fruit. Just as the oil embargo of 1973 had given Saudi Arabia a leadership role in the Arab world for the first time, it also created an intimate tie between a foreign policy issue and the Saudi populace. For the United States, the embargo took Saudi Arabia out of the category of curious, out-of-the-way places that happened to have valuable commodities and put it into the category of a potential threat to U.S. allies, global energy supplies, and U.S. ideals.

By the late 1970s U.S. policy toward Saudi Arabia had become something that had to be explained, and Saudi behavior had become something that had to be excused. To Saudis, this felt like a strategic ally was going soft. The peril became even more pointed after the Iranian Revolution of 1979, which collapsed a decade-long "Twin Pillar" strategy of U.S. support for Iran and Saudi Arabia to "fill the vacuum" left by Britain's withdrawal from the Gulf. The renewed Iranian threat and attempt to "export" the Iranian revolution made the Saudis once again agonize over their security. President Jimmy Carter committed U.S. forces to the defense of Persian Gulf oil in the aftermath of the Iranian revolution and the Soviet invasion of Afghanistan, but he had few forces to actually commit to that effort. The Carter Doctrine nonetheless signaled a strong U.S. commitment to the security of the Gulf. It was the Reagan administration that created those forces and gave substance to the U.S. commitment to Gulf security.

A new actor on the Saudi side also contributed to the deepening of U.S.-Saudi relations: an energetic and charismatic ambassador. Prince Bandar bin Sultan became the Saudi ambassador to Washington in 1983 and quickly made himself a darling of the Reagan administration with its vigorous anti-Soviet efforts by helping to fund adventures in Afghanistan and Latin America and later cautiously opening ties between Saudi Arabia and Jewish American groups (and later, Israel). This "extracurricular" assistance helped underline to American officials the strategic need for close ties to Saudi Arabia.

Still, the relationship was rocky. In 1981, Congress balked when President Ronald Reagan proposed selling radar surveillance planes known as AWACS (Airborne Warning and Control System) to Saudi Arabia, and the president scraped by after a long and difficult political battle with Congress.[16] The congressional battles have continued since, most recently with a proposed $20 billion arms sale in 2008 meant to steel Saudi Arabia and other Gulf allies against a threat from Iran. A group of 93 House members quickly objected to the inclusion of $123 million worth of precision-guided bombs.[17]

On internal security, U.S.-Saudi cooperation has been increasing dramatically—not so much after September 11, 2001, but more after May 12, 2003. On that date, and again on November 10, 2003, Saudi-based militants attacked foreigners' housing compounds in the Kingdom, killing dozens and sending a very clear signal that radical *jihadis* were a Saudi domestic problem and not merely a complication for Saudi foreign policy. The Saudi government embarked on a number of changes at home, ensuring that clerical voices fell into line, cutting funding for radical overseas activities, arresting scores, and imploring families to keep better track of their sons. But equally important, the United States dramatically improved its counterterror cooperation with Saudi Arabia, especially through the FBI, the U.S. State Department, and the U.S. Department of Treasury. Immediately following the May 2003 bombings in Riyadh, the FBI sent an investigative team to the Kingdom that cooperated with Saudi law enforcement and intelligence services to complete a thorough inquiry into the terrorist attack.[18] Although concern has lingered, U.S. officials publicly praised the greater security cooperation and Saudi counterterrorism efforts as well as specific Saudi steps such as the creation of a Financial Intelligence Unit (FIU).[19]

All of this suggests a vital role that the United States plays in security in Saudi Arabia—from without and from within. China cannot begin to play a similar role. At the same time, however, there is also a growing sense of grievance against the United States that a more developed Chinese relationship helps slake. Saudis feel particularly aggrieved that U.S. visa policy tightened so profoundly after 2001, not only requiring all Saudis to appear in person to apply for a visa, but denying visas to many (especially young men), subjecting the entire process to capricious timing and decisionmaking and subjecting many Saudis to secondary inspection or interrogation upon arrival in the United States. It is not coincidental, for example, that Saudi Aramco's annual training trip for up-and-coming managers in 2007 was held in China rather than the United States, in part to express displeasure over the persistent difficulties obtaining visas for Aramco engineers in years past.

Whereas the United States was the destination of choice for Saudi students abroad throughout the 1970s and 1980s, an increasing number are now moving to other English-speaking countries and to Asia. Some Saudis lament the shift, especially those who were educated and lived in the United States. A concerted push by the Kingdom has increased the number of Saudi scholarship students in U.S. institutions to a new high of more than 10,000—more than twice what it was in the wake of September 11.[20] Meanwhile, 400 Saudis now are slated to study in China, a number up from zero just a few years ago.[21]

WEAPONS SALES

Weapons sales have been an important part of Middle Eastern states' relations with both the United States and China. The region is one of the world's top consumers of arms. Overall, the seven highest defense spenders as a percentage of GDP are all in the Middle East, and a significant portion of this spending goes to arms purchases.[22] Although the Middle East arms market contracted from 2002 to 2005, it nonetheless accounted for 39 percent of all arms transfers in the developing world, and the top customers were Saudi Arabia, the UAE, Egypt, Israel, and Kuwait.[23] Weapons purchases have been a central component of defense strategies for the states of the Middle East, and the United States and China have been some of the leading providers of arms to the region. From 1995 to 2002, China supplied more than $1.2 billion dollars in military equipment to Iran, Algeria, Kuwait, and Libya.[24] Yet three metrics have generally informed the arms relationships: quality, price, and political constraints.

The quality of the weaponry flowing into (and out of) the Middle East has been a function of the technology, price, and seller. The United States possesses the world's best military technology, and the demand for U.S. defense products has traditionally been strong. From 2003 to 2006, the United States accounted for 38 percent of total arms transfers to the region, and much of it has been for high-quality products unavailable elsewhere (the percentage represented a significant drop from the previous five-year period, as Western European and Russian exports expanded).[25] China has rarely been a provider of high-tech weaponry to the Middle East, and the greater emphasis in recent years on advanced systems has hurt Chinese exports.

However, Chinese defense products have had an advantage over their U.S. rivals in price. Concerns about price are generally a reflection over budgets, and the region's poorer states may have been more inclined to purchase cheaper Chinese alternatives.

Finally, political constraints have been central in determining the flow of weapons into the Middle East. As consumers, there is a unanimous preference for simple commercial transactions that avoid political complications. The reality is that political concerns have played a major role at least in U.S. sales, and they have potentially made other partners more attractive. The relatively fewer political barriers that Middle Eastern consumers face in China may boost China's profile as a weapons provider to the region in the future, to the detriment of U.S. companies.

Yet given these metrics, no Middle Eastern state has opposed China's entrance into the weapons sales arena. States as diverse as Israel and Iran have sought to develop arms relationships with China, driven by the direct benefits to their militaries as well as the indirect political gains.

Aside from arms sales to Iran during the Iran-Iraq War, China has not become an alternative to the United States as a source of arms. Once the Iran-Iraq War was over, Russia quickly replaced China as Iran's preferred arms supplier. China has, however, occasionally served to remind U.S. officials that Saudi Arabia has alternatives to relying wholly on the United States for its weapons. In 1988, it was revealed that China sold Saudi Arabia 50 CSS-2 intermediate range ballistic missiles, which are capable of carrying a nuclear payload. Many in the United States viewed the act as a provocative one, and no Chinese deal of similar impact has been consummated since. Still, Saudi Arabia has become the third largest buyer of Chinese arms in the Middle East, lagging only behind Egypt and Iran.[26] Compared with sales by the United States, Russia, and European states, Chinese sales were minor (figure 3.4). Chinese arms were cheap and rugged, but so too were Russian arms. In terms of technological edge, European and U.S. weapons are superior to both, a fact that is recognized by Middle East defense procurement agencies.

IRAN

Like Saudi Arabia, Iran has welcomed the prospect of having China as a major energy partner and source of weapons. The relationship has the potential to grow. Bilateral trade between China and Iran, heavily weighted in favor of oil exports, rose from $4 billion to $7 billion between 2003 and 2004 alone, and by 2005 topped $10 billion according to the International Monetary Fund.[27] Yet Iran's motives differ from those of Saudi Arabia. Iran's oil sector is in desperate shape. Political isolation stemming from the Islamic Republic's involvement in international terrorism and, more recently, defiance of UN resolutions over its suspected nuclear program have hindered development of Iran's oil sector. Iran, which possesses the world's third-largest proven oil reserves (after Saudi Arabia and Canada), is the second-highest crude producer in OPEC after Saudi Arabia; yet, with the combined capacity of its refineries at 1.5 million bbl/d of crude oil, Iran must import nearly half its gasoline, which cost it $5 billion in 2006 alone.[28] The

Figure 3.4. Arms Deliveries to the Middle East* and North Africa, by Supplier, 1999–2006

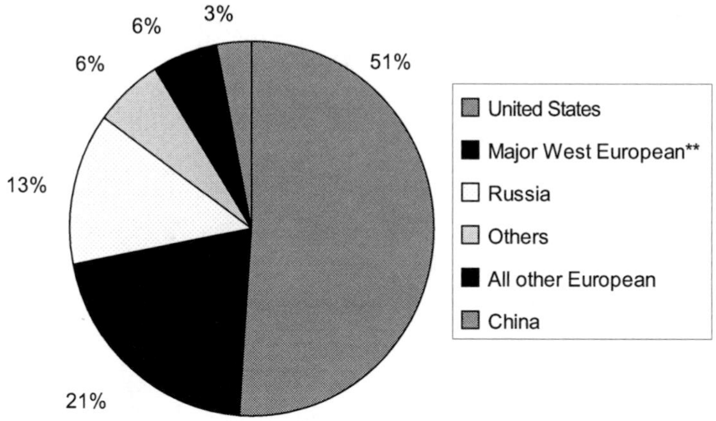

* Excluding Israel.
** Major West European countries includes UK, Germany, France, and Italy.
Source: CRS Report for Congress, Conventional Arms Transfers to Developing Nations, 1999–2006, September 26, 2007, 55, available at http://www.fas.org/asmp/resources/110th/RL34187.pdf.

inability of Iran to supply its domestic energy needs are a sign of the fundamental weakness of the Iranian regime.[29]

U.S. pressure on Iran, beginning toward the end of the Carter administration and slowly increasing over the last three decades, has helped steer international oil companies away from large-scale investments in Iran. The Iran-Libya Sanctions Act (ILSA) of 1996 threatened to impose penalties on individuals and foreign companies making significant investments in, or enhancements to, Iran's petroleum industry. That legislation, combined with the threat posed by bills such as the Iran Sanctions Enabling Act of 2007 (which would enable state pension funds to divest assets from companies investing in Iran's energy sector), has kept other countries and companies from fully committing to Iranian ventures. For example, in early 2004 the Japanese holding company INPEX (one-third owned by the government) cautiously agreed to a deal to help Iran's Petroleum Engineering and Development Company develop the southern Azadegan oil field in Iran. The billion-dollar investment had huge potential—perhaps 26 billion barrels of oil. Two years later, Japan relinquished almost all of its 75 percent stake in the field,[30] reportedly because of concerns about Iran's proliferation activities,[31] although it was clear that U.S. diplomatic pressure played a role. Reluctant international investment, the inability to draw international expertise to help recover difficult deposits, and soaring domestic demand growth for gasoline have all combined to cause Iran to miss its OPEC quota on oil exports for almost two years—at an annual cost of more than $5 billion.[32]

Deficiencies in Iranian supply and distribution were highlighted by disputes in early 2008 with Turkmenistan over pricing of natural gas. A cessation of Turkmen deliveries into Northern Iran led to a severe shortage and political embarrassment for President Ahmedinejad. In this highly unstable environment, Iran has heavily solicited Chinese technology and capital. At the same time China does not have a comparative advantage relative to the United States in enhanced oil recovery technologies needed to boost Iranian production in declining or underproducing fields.[33]

Iran has placed much hope in the ability of the China Petroleum and Chemical Corporation (Sinopec) to develop its natural gas reserves, which make up the world's second largest after Russia.[34] The capacity issue is particularly pressing, given poor internal gas distribution and related rows with Turkmenistan. In 2004, Sinopec signed a $70 billion memorandum of understanding with Iran under which Sinopec would buy 250 million tons of liquefied natural gas over 30 years and develop Iran's Yadavaran field, while Iran pledged to export 150,000 bbl/d of crude oil over 25 years.[35] China will continue to rely on energy imports to fuel its growth for years to come, making it an attractive market for Iranian producers.

China's noninterventionist foreign commercial policy is also a major plus for Iran's regime, which is under constant international pressure regarding human rights abuses. China's lack of direct concern with other countries' human rights problems is consistent with the way the Chinese would wish themselves to be treated, with regard to thorny issues such as Taiwan and Tibet. In a 2002 interview with *Asharq Alawsat*, China's deputy foreign minister for Taiwan, Hong Kong, and Macao affairs emphasized that his country would brook no foreign meddling in its internal affairs and would strongly resist any developments that threatened China's territorial integrity.[36] Included in the list of countries with poor human rights records with which China has had extensive commercial dealings are Iran, Libya, Burma, and notably Sudan, where Chinese have been accused of actively abetting the

Khartoum government in prosecuting genocide in Darfur, principally through arms sales.[37] On the occasion of the "restart" of a $2 billion contract with China's Sinopec to expand and develop Iran's Yadavaran field, Zhou Baixiu, Sinopec's director of international affairs and exploration, remarked at a news conference in Tehran: "If we had wanted to pay attention to this [American] pressure, we would not today have signed this agreement."[38]

Iran's post-revolutionary isolation on the international stage severely limited the number of willing arms sellers. Yet its needs have been great: it fought an extremely bloody eight-year war against Iraq, it has faced instability on its eastern border with Afghanistan for decades, and it has squared off against the United States and its Gulf allies since the revolution. Iran has needed weapons to supplement its conventional forces, many of which are rusting U.S. imports predating the revolution. Both the regular army and Revolutionary Guard need updated weapons to face the increasingly sophisticated militaries in the Arabian Gulf as well the continuing instability in Iraq and Afghanistan.

Yet political realities have continued to limit the availability of willing exporters, leaving Russia and China to fill much of the void. Compared to its neighbors, Iran has a major demographic advantage that slightly reduces its dependence on technology. Yet Iran lacks the budgetary surpluses of its Gulf neighbors and cannot as easily afford some of the most expensive items available to others, particularly at a time when it faces economic difficulties and the costs of a nuclear program.

Iran's recent history of weapons purchases confirms some of this. The Islamic Republic imported a range of tanks, missiles, and other items from China during its war with Iraq, including the Silkworm (HY-2), CS-801, and CS-802 anti-ship missiles.[39] China is also suspected of having produced several classes of tactical guided missiles "specifically for Iran," including JJ/TL-6bs and 10As, KJ/TL-10Bs, and a new variant of the C-107 anti-ship missile.[40]

IRAQ

Iraq holds some of the world's greatest underdeveloped energy reserves, but like Iran, political issues and a dearth of investment have slowed development of its fields. Iraq possesses the world's fourth-largest proven petroleum reserves, but many of its fields are significantly underdeveloped even though extraction costs are relatively low.[41] Although the majority of Iraq's oil exports go to Asian markets such as China, its total exports have been severely limited by the security constraints on its energy production and transportation infrastructure.[42] Following the Iraq War, oil production plummeted to 2 million bbl/d in 2006 from 2.6 million bbl/d in January 2003.[43] Even more than stable consumers, Iraq needs heavy investments in its energy infrastructure to raise production capacities.

Under Saddam Hussein and afterward, Iraq has sought to establish a strong energy relationship with China. China provides a major market for Iraqi oil and more important has been willing to invest in Iraqi oil fields. In June 2007 the China National Petroleum Company revived a contract it had originally signed with the previous Iraqi government in 1997 to develop the al-Ahdab field, whose estimated production capacity is 90,000 bbl/d.[44] In exchange, Chinese officials promised to cancel a large portion of Iraqi debt following a trip to China by Iraqi president Jalal Talabani. However, the political fight over the distribution of Iraqi oil wealth and continuing security challenges to the oil infrastructure have slowed the process. (The Iraqi-Chinese relationship is detailed in chapter 2.)

Yet it is the U.S. role in Iraq that will most likely shape the future of Iraq's energy sector. Iraq has been in talks with Chevron and ExxonMobil to develop a $3 billion petrochemical facility as well as with Dow Chemical and KBR to refurbish existing facilities.[45] Chevron and ExxonMobil are also in talks with Shell for possible projects to develop Iraqi energy fields,[46] and eight smaller U.S. energy companies have also signed production agreements with the Kurdistan Regional Government.[47]

A growing security relationship between the United States and Iraq is also likely, as the country's armed forces may inherit a portion of the U.S. hardware currently stationed there following any U.S. withdrawal. Already, its military has been significantly trained and equipped by the United States, and it is unlikely that these contacts will slow significantly in the near future. Yet China also has an arms relationship with Iraq, dating to Saddam Hussein's purchases during the Iran-Iraq War. These sales included a range of aircraft, missiles, tanks, and guns.[48]

ISRAEL

The depth and intricacy of the U.S.-Israeli relationship are hard to overstate. In 2007 the United States made a commitment of $30 billion in direct military aid over the next decade.[49] At the governmental level, military and intelligence cooperation is remarkably robust, as both the United States and Israel see themselves facing many of the same enemies. Bilateral trade is more than $27 billion a year, boosted by a 20-year-old free trade agreement.[50] The United States has been the principal arms supplier to Israel since the 1970s, and its hardware has helped make Israel's land and air forces superior to its neighbors. Israeli officials generally have direct access to the White House, and Israeli prime ministers are among its most frequent visitors. The relationship extends to state and local governments, and there has been a good deal of exchange between Israeli and local U.S. officials on both domestic security matters and trade issues.

The relationship is perhaps even more robust on the nonofficial level. More than half a million Americans visited Israel in 2007,[51] and a stunning one in every fifteen Israelis visited the United States in 2006.[52] The number of formal and informal ties between universities, businesses, and philanthropic organizations is truly mind-boggling and goes far beyond the American Jewish community. In addition, the rising support for Israel among Christian evangelicals in the United States and the almost universally strong support for Israel in the U.S. Congress broaden the base of that support far beyond its original enclaves in the northeastern United States. Israel is unique in its relations in the triangle as both a major consumer and supplier of weaponry. As a consumer, it has sought to maintain its qualitative edge over rivals by purchasing the highest-quality weapons available. Yet as a supplier, it has sought markets for its own domestically produced weapons. The tensions that have occasionally emerged between these goals have led to serious strains in Israel's relationships with both the United States and China.

Yet Israel's domestic arms industry exports 75 percent of its production, and Israel has actively sought to develop markets for its sophisticated weapons in China. This has sometimes brought U.S. military planners who take seriously the possibility of a U.S.-China war over Taiwan to oppose Israeli arms sales to China. In the 1980s, some analysts believe Israel covertly sold China as much as $4 billion in weapons before diplomatic relations were established in 1992.[53] These sales met little opposition from Washington at the time because Chinese military power during the 1980s was directed toward the Soviet Union, the Taiwan issue was quiet (with Taiwan being ruled by the "one China" Kuomintang), and Washington saw improved Sino-Israeli ties as a way of bringing China into closer alignment with the West. Tensions over Israel's China ties began rising in the 1990s as U.S.-PRC relations deteriorated, and the Taiwan issue emerged in virulent form with Taiwan's democratization and consequent drift away from China.

The United States forced Israel to withdraw from an earlier contract to sell four Phalcon aircraft to China in July 2000, for which Israel had to pay China $300 million in compensation.[54] U.S. defense officials feared that the Phalcon, a sophisticated Airborne Early Warning, Command and Control (AEWC&C) system, would change the strategic balance in the Taiwan Theater. Critics also alleged that China's Jian-10 fighter jet, a multi-role single-engine and single-seat tactical fighter airplane, integrated technology from Israel's now-defunct Lavi program, which had been seeded with $1.3 billion in U.S. aid.[55] A 2004 deal whereby Israel would upgrade and modernize China's Harpy armed drones collapsed under a fusillade of U.S. criticism, which included U.S. demands that Israel submit a written apology and that the director general of the Israeli Defense Ministry resign.[56] In 1999 and again in 2005, the United States insisted upon and won Israeli agreement that the United States would be notified about future arms deals with China.[57]

OTHER MIDDLE EASTERN COUNTRIES

Smaller Middle Eastern countries have been important consumers of weapons and other forms of security, and their small size often exacerbates their feelings of vulnerability. Much like Saudi Arabia, the primary external threats to the Gulf Cooperation Council (GCC) states since the 1990s have been Iraq and Iran, and the GCC has looked abroad for assistance in defending borders and regimes. Its geostrategic importance is unquestioned as well, as 50 tankers on a daily average pass through the Straits of Hormuz carrying 25 percent of global oil supply.[58] Given its geographical location, however, few nonregional militaries can apply overwhelming force in a relevant time frame. From the Gulf perspective, the United States has been the obvious choice to fill this role. Its power projection capabilities are unrivaled, as its navy can effectively secure the Gulf for shipping and its air force provides a credible deterrent. The two U.S.-led Gulf wars saw the full application of U.S. military strength, as naval and air forces covered a large-scale ground operation. More recently, the U.S. Navy has maintained a permanent carrier presence in the Gulf based in Bahrain and for much of 2007 had an additional carrier group deployed there as well. The U.S. Navy can also deploy three more carriers to the Gulf within three weeks of being called up.[59]

Although the GCC perceives a need for protection against ambitious neighbors, China cannot play a direct role. Some would argue that China's entry into the Gulf would violate its own principle that the security affairs of the Gulf should be handled by the states littoral to that body of water and not by external actors. Regardless, the Gulf's Arab states need credible deterrents, and China simply does not possess the land, naval, or air forces to accomplish this in the Gulf currently. The construction of the port in Gwadar, Pakistan, along with the construction of railways between Western China and Iran, plus the steady improvement of the Sino-Pakistan highway over the Karakorum Mountains, may speed the timeline for China to achieve significant power projection capabilities, but even then Chinese forces remain decades behind their U.S. counterparts. Although not as large or significant as Iran, Saudi Arabia, or Israel's arms relationships with the United States or China, other states in the region have sought to develop their military to military cooperation as well. Gulf states like the United Arab Emirates (UAE) and Qatar have built their air forces with imports of advanced U.S. warplanes including the F-16.[60] There is also speculation that the F-22 may at some point be sold to the U.S. Gulf allies, particularly as multiple firms compete to sell advanced training aircraft to the UAE.[61] The recent $20 billion arms package from the United States to the Gulf includes a range of antimissile systems and aircraft, as well as additional missiles for the UAE and Kuwait.[62] The U.S. role at this point dwarfs China's in supplying the Gulf states, although there remains potential for a greater Chinese role in the future.

NONENERGY TRADE

Beyond energy and security, the China–Middle East commercial relationship is growing to include a range of industrial and consumer goods. As for producers throughout the world, China is an extremely attractive market for Middle Eastern products, given its demographic weight and growing consumer class. Industrial initiatives throughout the Gulf that require high energy inputs seek to tap into China's high-growth construction market. China has also become a significant exporter to the Middle East, providing the region with cheap manufactured goods and filling its shops with commercial products. Total exports to the Middle East (excluding Morocco, Algeria, and Tunisia) were estimated to top $33 billion in 2006.[63] The awesome potential for greater nonenergy trade ahead has led Middle Eastern states to embrace China as a strategic trading partner.

Exports to China

In 2006, total GCC-China trade stood at more than $40 billion, the vast majority of which was Middle Eastern hydrocarbon exports to China.[64] More broadly total Chinese trade with the Middle East exceeded $76 billion (figure 3.5).[65] Although bilateral trade with China has increased throughout the Middle East, nonenergy trade has grown in relative and absolute terms, though still representing a relatively small share of the region's overall trade with China.

Middle East producers, the GCC in particular, have sought to take advantage of China's massive market, ongoing construction boom, and appetite for raw materials more broadly. China's demand for aluminum, for example, is predicted to rise 20 percent annually until 2010.[66] The Gulf is well placed to meet this demand, as local production of the metal has increased dramatically, with the number of aluminum extrusion presses (key inputs in aluminum production) rising from 25 to 85 in the Middle East in 2007 alone. Although 90 percent of product goes to the local construction sector, much of the surplus capacity is exported to Asian markets.[67]

Chemical and petrochemical manufacturing has flourished in the GCC as well. The Saudi Basic Industries Corporation (SABIC) exports $2 billion annually to China of goods like fertilizers, synthetic fabrics, iron, steel, and plastics.[68] Following Chinese president Hu Jintao's April 2006 visit to Saudi Arabia, Sinopec and SABIC, the largest chemical production company in Saudi Arabia, signed a joint venture agreement to create an ethylene derivative production facility in Tianjin, Northern China. Sinopec will invest US$1.7 billion in the venture, scheduled to open in fall 2009.[69]

Figure 3.5. Chinese Trade with the Middle East

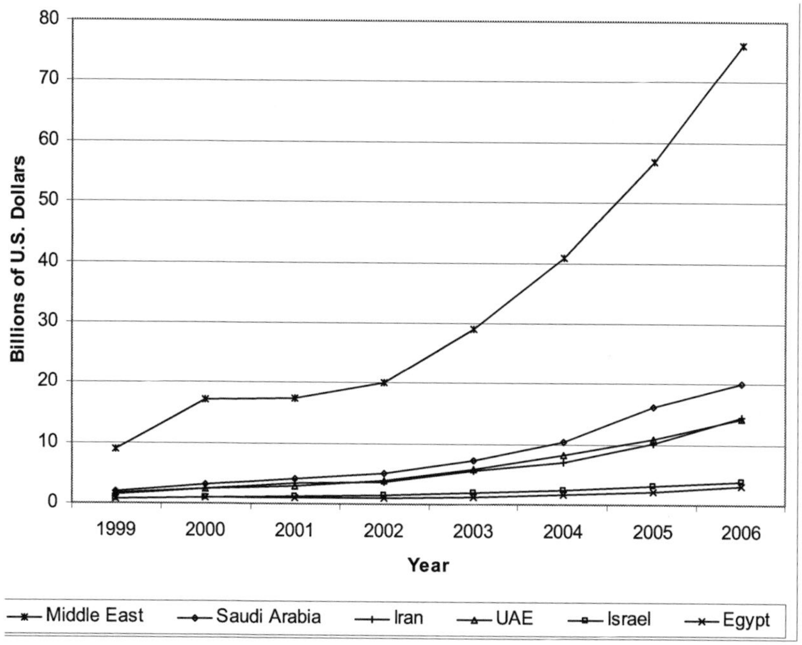

Source: International Monetary Fund, *Direction of Trade Statistics Yearbook 2006,* 135, and *Direction of Trade Statistics Quarterly December 2007,* 96–97.

Imports from China

The composition of China–Middle East trade is very much consistent with the Chinese strategy of using comparatively cheap labor to produce low-cost goods, from ready-to-wear fashion to cars, in abundance (figure 3.6). To cite a few examples, in early 2004, a significant amount of consumer goods on the Libyan market were of Chinese origin, reflecting trends elsewhere in the region (the value of official Chinese exports to Libya rose from $216 million in 2003 to $1.3 billion in 2005).[70] Egypt projects that China will replace the United States as its largest trading partner as early as 2012 and is aiming to increase its share of Chinese exports and reexports to Europe through the Suez Canal by lowering transit fees.[71] The Middle East also constitutes a major market for Chinese car and motorcycle exports, which have grown dramatically since 2000.[72] According to the World Trade Organization, China exported to the Middle East (excluding North Africa) $1.35 billion in automotive

Figure 3.6. Chinese Exports to the Middle East, by Product Type, 2006

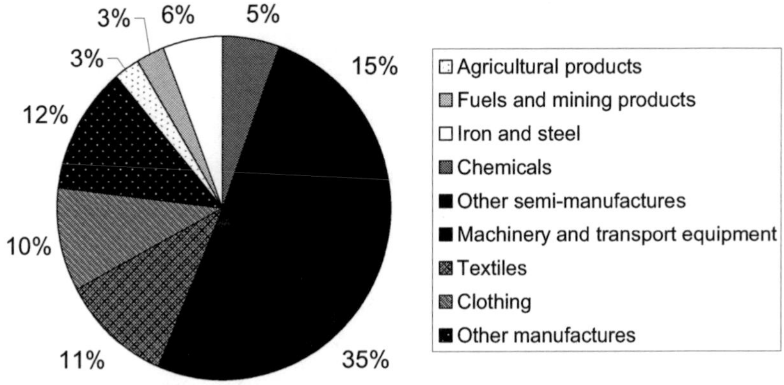

Source: World Trade Organization, International Trade Statistics 2007, Appendix table A22, available at http://www.wto.org/english/res_e/statis_e/its2007_e/its07_toc_e.htm.

parts, part of $2.19 billion in transportation equipment including motorcycles.[73] To help meet its goal of bringing Middle East trade to $100 billion by 2010, from $51.3 billion in 2005,[74] China has been investing heavily in marketing infrastructure. The UAE is quickly becoming one of China's most important trading partners in the Middle East, and there are reports of Chinese goods flooding UAE markets. There are more than 1,000 Chinese companies in the UAE, and the emirate of Dubai is home to "Dragon Mart," a 150,000 square mile mall and one of the largest regional showcases of Chinese consumer goods. The mall sports 150,000 square meters of consumer-goods.[75]

Putting this trade somewhat in perspective, U.S. imports from China in 2006 were approximately $288 billion, against $55 billion in exports (for a balance of trade of $233 billion in China's favor).[76] Excluding the UAE, U.S. exports to the Middle East rose 57 percent between 2001 and 2006, while China-GCC trade over the last few years has risen more than 33 percent annually.[77] These statistics highlight both the recent, rapid growth of Middle East–China trade as well as the fact that, given the sheer size of the U.S. export market, China cannot afford to leave relations with the United States out of its regional decision calculus.

In perspective, U.S. nonmilitary exports to the Middle East include a range of machinery, vehicles, electronics, and assorted commercial goods. The UAE is the largest U.S. export market in the Arab world, and exports of U.S. goods to the UAE increased by 352 percent between 2001 and 2006 alone (from $2.6 billion to $11.9 billion).[78]

Capital Flows

The Middle East is both a supplier and recipient of capital. As a supplier, it seeks markets that promise the highest returns, and the recent boom in oil prices has made the GCC states the biggest capital-holders in the Middle East. Official reserves in the GCC countries are expected to balloon from $51 billion in 2002 to $150 billion in 2012, and total current-account surpluses in the GCC already stand at more than $200 billion.[79] Local markets are unable to absorb that much capital without incurring inflation and social instability, so instead they have looked abroad. The United States has historically been the obvious choice for this money, given its large market filled with relatively wealthy consumers, solid legal framework, and liquidity. More recently, sovereign wealth funds have been the highest-profile tools for Gulf investments. In November 2007 the Abu Dhabi Investment Authority (ADIA) purchased a $7.5 billion stake in Citigroup following the U.S. mortgage crisis.[80] The Kuwait Investment Authority (KIA) was also in a group of investors that purchased $6.6 billion in Merrill Lynch's stock.[81] U.S. markets remain attractive to Gulf investors, yet the public and congressional concerns that have emerged over these investments have raised flags for Gulf investors over the future of the U.S. market. Following the failed Dubai Ports World deal in 2006, Gulf investors have referred to a "political risk premium" of investing in the United States.

Compared to the 1970s, though, Gulf investors are also more interested in moving away from the safety of U.S. Treasury bills toward opportunities for greater returns and direct management of assets.[82] GCC investors in this regard see China as a particularly promising prospect for investment, given the high returns possible there. One high-profile example is the Kuwait Investment Authority's purchase of $720 million worth of shares in the Industrial and Commercial Bank of China (ICBC)—China's largest bank.[83] In announcing the purchase, KIA's managing director noted that "this participation demonstrates Kuwait's deepening economic ties with China as well as showcases the long term strategic value of KIA as a core investor. This participation also marks the beginning of KIA's long term strategic investment plan in China, which KIA hopes to extend to many other sectors."[84] The Qatar Investment Authority also invested

$206 million in ICBC, and the bank will be opening a branch in Doha and is planning another in Dubai.[85]

Yet parts of the Middle East are consumers of capital as well, particularly the energy-poor states in the Levant and North Africa. Jordan, for example, has opened its first car manufacturing plant. Hebei Zhongxing Automobile of China has partnered with the Iyas Company for Manufacturing Automobiles and the Jordan Investment Board to build a $30 million facility producing cars for sale to Arab and Eastern European markets.[86] Additionally, Jordanian engineers will train in China as part of the agreement and then return to manage the local plant.[87] In Egypt, the China Export-Import Bank granted a $16.3 million loan to the Egyptian Holding Company for Cotton Spinning and Weaving to refurbish a polyester factory, as well as a $20 million loan to renovate the Cairo International Conference Centre (CICC) and build its hotel.[88] The Citic Group, China's largest state-owned company, also plans to invest $800 million in an aluminum plant in Ismailia, most of whose output will go to China.[89] Aluminum of China (Chalco), China's largest aluminum producer, signed an agreement in October 2007 with Malaysian and Saudi partners to build a $3 billion aluminum facility in Saudi Arabia.[90]

Finally, the China National Chemical Engineering Company (CNCEC) with the Al-Kharafi group of Kuwait plans to construct a $700 million chemical plant in Fayoum, Egypt.[91]

POLITICS

China's most delicate role to play in the Middle East may not be in the areas of trade and industry, in which it has excelled, but rather in politics. However much Beijing may seek to stay out of the thicket of Middle Eastern diplomacy, its increasingly large role and the rising expectations that regional actors have for the utility of Chinese involvement may make further involvement unavoidable. Part of the impetus to treat China differently may be a consequence of its diplomatic cunning up to now. All parties see China as potentially friendly, and as Abdulaziz Sager of the Gulf Research Center noted, "the chief advantage of China's role in the region is its lack of political baggage."[92]

Arab-Israeli Peace Process

External actors have historically played a significant role in the Arab-Israeli and Israeli-Palestinian peace processes. Local actors have often sought superpower support to advance their own positions and mediate, but there has rarely been consensus over which state should play this role and the appropriate functions for such a state. The United States has filled some version of this role, but its actions have often generated criticism as well: by Arab states, which accuse the United States of being partial toward Israel or too disengaged from the process, and by Israelis, who accuse some Americans of not fully appreciating their security environment. China has started from a marginal position and has often gotten high marks for its efforts. It has stayed out of the political fray by consistently supporting a peaceful resolution of the conflict through negotiations based on previous United Nations resolutions.[93]

Across the range of actors, from Israel to the Western-aligned Sunni states to rejectionist states like Syria and Iran, China's recent entrance into Arab-Israeli affairs has been met with some acclaim. During Chinese president Jiang Zemin's trip to the Middle East in 2000, Yasser Arafat directly requested that China appoint a permanent special envoy for the region,[94] and China did so. At one point it also flirted with the idea of joining the international "quartet" working on Israeli-Palestinian issues—a group that includes the United States, the European Union, Russia, and the UN—but by late 2006, that effort seemed to have been largely abandoned.[95] In the aftermath of the 2006 Lebanon war, Premier Wen Jiabao announced that China would increase its forces in the United Nations Interim Force in Lebanon (UNIFIL) to 1,000. Chinese forces included an engineering battalion and medical team that were involved in demining as well as UNIFIL's broader mission of patrolling Southern Lebanon.[96] China has so far maintained about 335 peacekeepers in Lebanon as of the end of 2007. Nonetheless there is little direct evidence at the moment that China seeks a central role in Arab-Israeli diplomacy.

Iranian Nuclear Issue

Just as they have welcomed Chinese input into the Arab-Israeli Peace Process, Middle Eastern states are receptive to a greater Chinese role in resolving the standoff over Iran's alleged nuclear weapons program.

The notion of a nuclear-armed Shi`ite state is of particular concern to the Sunni mainstream, particularly neighboring Gulf states. As recent history has shown, China's relations with Iran are dictated by an ambivalence that stems from firm economic interests, tempered (but not controlled) by what is likely a genuine desire to slow—if not obviate—regional nuclear proliferation.[97] (This issue is addressed in chapter 2.)

Iran is keen to play the energy card with China to influence international policy: As a permanent member of the UN Security Council, China's ability to veto (or at least, to threaten to veto) potential new resolutions against Iran is a powerful asset. Alhough it has voted in favor of a number of Security Council resolutions sanctioning Iran, China has also consistently worked to water them down. So far, this lack of decisive support from China (and Russia) on the Iran nuclear issue has in part, blocked efforts to build an international consensus for imposing tougher sanctions on Iran.[98] Any expressed Chinese and Russian concerns regarding an increasingly intransigent Iranian stance on uranium enrichment should be weighed against both countries' support for Iran's enrichment program through sales of critical technology, dating back more than 10 years.[99] In the Chinese case, though there is likely low-level cooperation, it is not as visible or vital as Russian cooperation, nor is it detailed in open sources. Many Sunni Arab states, and certainly Israel, would welcome activist Chinese participation in efforts to control Iran's nuclear program.

Internal Reform

External pressure for political reform in the Middle East has generated significant concern among Arab regimes. Not only has the Iraqi example been particularly frightful, but no regime is anxious to open space for opposition movements that may threaten its power. President Bush's "freedom agenda" has been the embodiment of this U.S. effort, and U.S. Arab allies and enemies alike have sought to block its effectiveness. Although the particularities of individual regimes may differ, there is widespread agreement amongst Arab states that U.S. pressure for reform is unwelcome.

Beyond this opposition to U.S. democracy efforts is an appreciation of China's avowed disinterest in Arab reform. Arab regimes and intellectuals alike hold China as a model: it is a lucrative trading partner and objective observer in international affairs, but absent in their domestic politics. China makes no claims on Arab regimes as to their treatment of the opposition, human rights, or elections, nor is it in the CCP's interest ever to do so.

CULTURAL LINKS

Public opinion polls have borne out the precipitous decline of the U.S. standing in the Middle East. Although the causes for this shift are still debated, the succession of the Palestinian issue and two U.S.-led wars (in Iraq and Afghanistan) have largely paralleled the downturn. Strikingly, publics even in U.S. allies like Jordan, Egypt, and Morocco have grown sour about the U.S. role in the Middle East and the state of its relationships with local regimes. Whether this changes with the introduction of a new administration or new policies is unclear, but the recent trend has been undeniable.

In a 2006 Arab public opinion survey conducted by Shibley Telhami and Zogby International, 78 percent of respondents listed their views of the United States as either somewhat or very unfavorable.[100] Jordan, Saudi Arabia, and Morocco, all U.S. allies in the region, had the highest percentages of very unfavorable views of the United States. Similarly, Jordan, Egypt, and Morocco had the lowest confidence ratings in the United States.

On the other side, 9/11 has made some Americans increasingly skeptical about the U.S. relationship with allies such as Saudi Arabia. Stringent new visa requirements and screening of Arab travelers have made visiting the United States more frustrating, and an increasing number of Arabs are looking to universities in Britain, Australia, and New Zealand because of easier visa processes.[101] Similarly, congressional opposition to the Dubai Ports World deal in early 2006 and recent fears about Arab sovereign wealth fund investments have increased apprehensions in the Middle East.[102] Overall, as more Arabs doubt their prospects for visiting or studying in the United States, fewer personal connections are being forged.

Conversely, Middle Eastern views of China have risen dramatically in recent years. In the same Telhami/Zogby International poll, respondents ranked China second after France as the country they would most like to be a superpower in a world with only one superpower.[103] Part of this is that China's profile in the Middle East has been able to develop without serious historical frictions between them.

China is both new to the Middle East and offers an inspiring model for how an ancient civilization can grow and prosper in the modern era. Arab intellectuals have particularly seized upon this point, and numerous articles and statements have identified China's path to modernization as worth studying for the Arabs. Naguib Mahfouz argued that Arab societies should diversify what they borrow from abroad to include lessons from China, whose historical and social traditions resemble the Middle East's more closely.[104] An author writing recently in an Emirati newspaper suggested that the "China Model" proves "there is another pathway for governments of the world to follow in order to successfully pursue economic growth."[105] Abdel-Moneim Said of the Al-Ahram Centre for Political and Strategic Studies in Cairo noted the discrepancies between Arab and Chinese responses to grave social challenges and concluded that China's path to development had something to offer Arabs.[106]

The increased public and elite interest in China has manifested itself in growing educational and tourist links. Centers for Sino-studies in the Middle East are multiplying. Ain Shams University hosts the largest Chinese department in Africa with 500 undergraduate Chinese majors, while Al-Azhar hosts 200 students of Chinese.[107] Cairo University also launched its own China program in 2004 with China's vice minister of education in attendance for the opening ceremony, and the Chinese government donated 1,000 Chinese-language books and magazines to support the department.[108] In 2005, Egyptian and Chinese education officials agreed to establish the "Egyptian Chinese University" in Cairo, making it the first Chinese university in the Middle East.[109] In Saudi Arabia as well, Saudi students are studying directly in China on scholarships awarded by Chinese companies operating in Saudi Arabia.[110] The Chinese government is also offering scholarships directly to students and professionals for further training.[111]

Tourist links are set to grow as well. The number of Chinese tourists is predicted to reach 100 million by 2015, creating a lucrative market that Arab businesses hope to reach.[112] The Egyptian Tourism Authority is basing part of its future tourism strategy on attracting Chinese tourists.[113] An agreement signed in October 2001 to open Egypt to Chinese tourists enabled 35,000 Chinese to visit Egypt in 2005, a number expected to grow to 65,000 in coming years.[114] Chinese tourism to Dubai more than doubled between 2004 and 2006 simply upon the introduction of direct flights by Emirates Airlines.[115] Although still relatively small, the amount of personal contact between Chinese and

Arabs looks to grow exponentially in coming decades, which could form the basis for more strategic relationships.

CONCLUSION

The Middle East has looked to the United States for security and trade ties for decades, and that is unlikely to change soon. The states of the GCC continue to feel the need for a superpower patron with the military capabilities to defend their regimes and protect their energy exports. The states of the Levant all recognize that the United States will play a role in any Arab-Israeli and Israeli-Palestinian peace process. Iraq will need U.S. defense and political support, while the GCC states will seek U.S. protection from Iranian depredations and North Africa's states will continue to build their trade relationships with the United States.

Yet, although the United States may remain dominant for the foreseeable future, the states of the Middle East are unanimously trying to broaden and deepen their ties with China, albeit for sometimes different reasons. The Gulf states recognize China as one of the world's primary drivers for growing energy demand; Iran needs Chinese support for developing its oil fields; and the Middle East's nonenergy states are seeking Chinese investment. For all these countries, developing stronger ties with China provides useful leverage in their own relations with the United States.

As the states of the Middle East build their relationships with China, they will need to remain vigilant to the ups and downs in the U.S.-China relationship. Especially for those states actively developing ties with China in order to shape their own bilateral relationship with the United States, the balancing act could become highly unstable if Middle Eastern states misread tensions between the two powers. Israel, which has spent decades studying U.S. politics, has already stumbled in this process and created lasting concern in Washington over its intentions with China.

The Middle East is seeking to integrate China in a way that makes China an asset for regional stability, and the process has been uncertain thus far. States hostile to the United States seem eager to encourage a Sino-American rivalry, or at the very least to encourage China to circumvent international efforts at isolation and punishment. Were China to accede to such efforts, the consequences almost certainly would be a stepped-up U.S. presence in the region, heightened instability, and resultant consequence for the Sino-American relationship more broadly. Interestingly, however, there is a good deal of room for China to build deeper ties with the Middle East, and a large number of opportunities to make small but significant contributions to regional security. China's rising role will almost certainly entail moving beyond the narrow commercial confines in which China seems most comfortable, but Chinese diplomacy in the region appears to be growing increasingly sophisticated and able to maneuver the dangerous shoals that have trapped foreign powers in the region for more than a century.

Notes

1. For an interesting description of the Soviet role in the midst of the Cold War, see George Lenczowski, *Soviet Advances in the Middle East* (Washington, D.C.: American Enterprise Institute for Public Policy Research, 1972), *passim.*

2. The leading study on China's role in the Middle East during the Cold War remains Yitzhak Shichor, *The Middle East in China's Foreign Policy* (Cambridge: Cambridge University Press, 1979). See also Hashim S.H. Behbehani, *China's Foreign Policy in the Arab World, 1955–1975* (London: Kegan Paul, 1981), and Lillian Craig Harris, *China Considers the Middle East* (London: I.B. Tauris and Co, 1993) and P.R. Kumaraswamy, *China and the Middle East: The Quest for Influence* (Thousand Oaks, Calif.: Sage Publications, 1999).

3. *Inter alia,* President Bush called for energy independence in his 2003 State of the Union Address; the Energy Independence and Security Act of 2007, signed into law December 19, 2007, explicitly tied together the two concepts.

4. Thomas Friedman, "The New Red, White and Blue," *New York Times*, January 6, 2006, http://select.nytimes.com/2006/01/06/opinion/06friedman.html.

5. Reuters, "Saudi Royal says US Oil Independence a Myth," February 25, 2007, http://www.reuters.com/article/politicsNews/idUSL2522428620070225.

6. Transcript of "The Other Opinion," *Al Jazeera*, October 2, 2006, www.aljazeera.net (in Arabic).

7. David Winning, "Saudi Arabia Remains China's Top Crude Supplier," *Marketwatch*, January 22, 2008, http://www.marketwatch.com/news/story/saudi-arabia-remains-chinas-top/story.aspx?guid=%7BA1CC9784-BE88-48B3-8B8F-656EC654EB6C%7D.

8. Energy Information Administration, "Country Analysis Briefs: Saudi Arabia," February 2007, http://www.eia.doe.gov/emeu/cabs/Saudi_Arabia/pdf.pdf.

9. Ibid.

10. Energy Information Administration, "Saudi Arabia: Oil Exports and Shipping," February 2007, http://www.eia.doe.gov/cabs/Saudi_Arabia/OilExports .html.

11. "Saudi Aramco to Press Ahead with Yanbu' Refinery and Heavy Oil Development," *APS Review Gas Market Trends*, October 8, 2007, http://www .entrepreneur.com/tradejournals/article/169688443.html.

12. Winning, "Saudi Arabia Remains China's Top Crude Supplier."

13. "Saudi Aramco to Press Ahead."

14. Energy Information Administration, "Crude Oil and Total Petroleum Imports Top 15 Countries," March 3, 2008, http://www.eia.doe.gov/pub/oil _gas/petroleum/data_publications/company_level_imports/current/import .html.

15. Nadav Safran, *Saudi Arabia: The Ceaseless Quest for Security* (Ithaca: Cornell University Press, 1985, 1988), 295–296.

16. Jeff Gerth, "81 Saudi Deal: Help for Rebels for U.S. Arms," *New York Times*, February 4, 1987, http://query.nytimes.com/gst/fullpage.html?res=9B 0DE2DC1038F937A35751C0A961948260.

17. Associated Press, "Lawmakers Want to Keep Bombs from Saudis," February 13, 2008, http://abcnews.go.com/Politics/wireStory?id=4289209.

18. John Pistole, "Terrorism Financing: Origination, Organization, and Prevention," testimony before Senate Committee on Governmental Affairs, July 31, 2003, http://www.fbi.gov/congress/congress03/pistole073103.htm.

19. See 9/11 commission report. See also Alfred Prado and Christopher Blanchard, "Saudi Arabia: Current Issues and US Relations," Congressional Research Service, August 2, 2006, http://fas.org/sgp/crs/mideast/RL33533 .pdf.

20. Caryle Murphy and Susan Kinzie, "Saudis Again Head to U.S. Campuses," *Washington Post*, November 11, 2006, http://www.washingtonpost.com/ wp-dyn/content/article/2006/11/10/AR2006111001628.html.

21. Xiao Wang, "Close Ties with China Set to Intensify Further," *China Daily*, September 22, 2007, http://www.chinadaily.com.cn/cndy/2007-09/22/ content_6125953.htm.

22. The top 7 spenders in order are Oman, Qatar, Saudi Arabia, Iraq, Jordan, Israel, and Yemen. "Rank Order–Military expenditures–percent of GDP," *CIA World Factbook*, March 6, 2008, https://www.cia.gov/library/publications/ the-world-factbook/rankorder/2034rank.html.

23. "China's Middle East Military Market," *Jane's Islamic Affairs*, July 1, 2007, http://www8.janes.com/Search/documentView.do?docId=/content1/

janesdata/mags/jiaa/history/jiaa2007/jiaa5067.htm@current&pageSelected
=allJanes&keyword=china%20saudi%20arms&backPath=http://search.janes
.com/Search&Prod_Name=JIAA&/.

24. Richard Grimmett, "Conventional Arms Transfers to Developing Nations, 1995–2002," Congressional Research Service, September 22, 2003, 59, http://www.fas.org/man/crs/RL32084.pdf.

25. "China's Middle East Military Market," *Jane's Islamic Affairs.*

26. Between 2002 and 2005, the top recipients of Chinese arms in order were Egypt, Iran, and Saudi Arabia. See ibid.

27. International Monetary Fund (IMF), *Direction of Trade Statistics Yearbook 2006* (Washington, D.C.: IMF, 2006), 135.

28. Energy Information Administration, "Country Analysis Briefs: Iran," October 2007, http://www.eia.doe.gov/emeu/cabs/Iran/pdf.pdf.

29. Ibid.

30. Islamic Republic News Agency, "Inpex of Japan gives concession to NIOC on Azadegan oil field," October 8, 2006, http://www.irna.com/en/news/view/menu-234/0610089712171003.htm.

31. "Iran Oil Firm Head Reluctant to Extend Azadegan Deadline," *Japan Times*, October 4, 2006, http://search.japantimes.co.jp/cgi-bin/nb20061004a3.html.

32. Roger Stern, "The Iranian Petroleum Crisis and United States National Security," *Proceedings of the National Academy of Sciences*, January 2, 2007, http://www.pnas.org/cgi/reprint/0603903104v1.pdf.

33. U.S. Department of State, *Doing Business in Libya: A Country Commercial Guide for U.S. Companies*, March 2006, http://www.buyusa.gov/egypt/en/libya_country_commercial_guide.pdf.

34. EIA, "Country Analysis Briefs: Iran."

35. "China, Iran Sign Biggest Oil and Gas Deal," *China Daily*, October 31, 2004, http://www.chinadaily.com.cn/english/doc/2004-10/31/content_387140.htm.

36. "Musaid Wazir al Harijiyya as-Sini: Taddahul al Askari Warid fi Taiwan Ithan Taarrudat Wihdat as-Sin Lil Khatar," *Asharq Alawsat*, October 26, 2002.

37. BBC News, "China Defends Arms Sales to Sudan," Feburary 22, 2008, http://news.bbc.co.uk/2/hi/asia-pacific/7258059.stm.

38. "Sinopec and the Iran National Oil Company (NOC) Sign a US2 Billion Deal to Expand Iranian Oil Infrastructure," (Farsi), *Hamshahri*, December 11, 2007.

39. "China's Middle East Military Market."

40. Dan Blumenthal, "Providing Arms: China and the Middle East," *The Middle East Quarterly* (Spring 2005), http://www.meforum.org/article/695.

41. Energy Information Administration, "Country Analysis Briefs: Iraq," August 2007, http://www.eia.doe.gov/emeu/cabs/Iraq/pdf.pdf.

42. Ibid.

43. Ibid..

44. Jamil Anderlini and Steve Negus, "Iraq Revives Saddam deal with China," *Financial Times*, June 22, 2007, http://www.ft.com/cms/s/0/c6c6f958 -2108-11dc-8d50-000b5df10621.html.

45. Spencer Swartz, "Iraq in Talks with Chevron, Exxon," Associated Press, January 25, 2007, http://www.ibtimes.com/articles/20070125/add1-iraq-chevron -exxon_1.htm.

46. United Press International, "Exxon, Shell: Iraq Oil Law Needed for Deal," February 13, 2008, http://www.upi.com/International_Security/Energy/ Briefing/2008/02/13/exxon_shell_iraq_oil_law_needed_for_deal/9680/.

47. "Iraq: Kurds, Foreigners, and Oil," Strategic Forecasting, Inc., January 22, 2008, http://www.stratfor.com/analysis/iraq_kurds_foreigners_and_oil.

48. Daniel Byman and Roger Cliff, *China's Arms Sales: Motivations and Implications* (Washington D.C.: Rand, 1999), http://www.rand.org/pubs/mono-graph_reports/MR1119/MR1119.appa.pdf.

49. Steven Erlanger, "Israel to Get $30 Billion in Military Aid from U.S.," *New York Times*, August 17, 2007, http://www.nytimes.com/2007/08/17/ world/middleeast/17israel.html.

50. Richard Jones, "Remarks by Ambassador Richard H. Jones at Chamber Event, July 2, 2007," Israel-America Chamber of Commerce, July 2, 2007, http://www.amcham.co.il/main/siteNew/index.php?page=39&action=sidLin k&stId=335.

51. Associated Press, "American Tourism to Israel Breaks Old Record," January 27, 2008, http://www.newsday.com/travel/ny-c5549283jan27,0,3397104.story.

52. "Haaretz Interview: Director General Israel Hernandez," http://www .buyusa.gov/israel/en/dg_interview.html.

53. Sudha Ramachandran, "US up in Arms over Sino-Israel Ties," *Asia Times*, December 21, 2004, http://www.atimes.com/atimes/Middle_East/ FL21Ak01.html.

54. Dan Blumenthal, "Providing Arms: China and the Middle East."

55. Doug Tsuruoka, "With J-10, China Finally on Course in Military Export Field," GlobalSecurity.org, April 3, 2007, http://www.globalsecurity.org/ org/news/2007/070403-china-export.htm. See also David Isenberg, "Israel's Role in China's New Airplane," *Asia Times*, December 4, 2002, http://www .atimes.com/atimes/China/DL04Ad01.html.

56. Arye O'Sullivan, "Pentagon Fuming over Arms Sale to China," *Jerusalem Post*, December 16, 2004.

57. Scott Wilson, "Israel Set to End China Arms Deal under U.S. Pressure," *Washington Post*, June 27, 2005, http://www.washingtonpost.com/wp-dyn/content/article/2005/06/26/AR2005062600544.html.

58. Tim Ripley, "Gulf of Distrust—Naval Stand-offs and the Persian Gulf," *Jane's Intelligence Review*, March 1, 2008, http://www4.janes.com/subscribe/jir/doc_view.jsp?K2DocKey=/content1/janesdata/mags/jir/history/jir2008/jir10335.htm@current&Prod_Name=JIR&.

59. Ibid.

60. "Emirati Air Force," GlobalSecurity.org, http://www.globalsecurity.org/military/world/gulf/uae-af.htm.

61. "President-elect Lee Solicits UAE to Pick Korean Trainer Jet," Korea .net, January 9, 2008, http://www.korea.net/news/news/newsView.asp?serial_no=20080109019&part=102&SearchDay=&page=1.

62. "Reflecting Change: 2007 Annual Defence Report," *Jane's Defence Weekly*, December 26, 2007, http://www4.janes.com/subscribe/jdw/doc_view .jsp?K2DocKey=/content1/janesdata/mags/jdw/history/jdw2007/jdw35118 .htm@current&Prod_Name=JDW&QueryText=%3CAND%3E(%3COR%3 E((%5B80%5D(+world+%3CAND%3E+defense+%3CAND%3E+spending) +%3CIN%3E+body)%2C+(%5B100%5D+(%5B100%5D(+world+%3CAND %3E+defense+%3CAND%3E+spending)+%3CIN%3E+title)+%3CAND%3E +(%5B100%5D(+world+%3CAND%3E+defense+%3CAND%3E+spending) +%3CIN%3E+body)))).

63. The International Monetary Fund does not include Morocco, Algeria, or Tunisia as part of the Middle East. IMF, *Direction of Trade Statistics Quarterly December 2007*, 96–97.

64. "With cash to burn, China and Mideast eye each other's riches," *Financial Times*, September 6, 2007, http://search.ft.com/ftArticle?queryText =China+and+GCC+trade&y=0&aje=true&x=0&id=070906000687&ct=0. See also Daniel Stanton, "Delegates Push for Closer Ties between GCC and China," ArabianBusiness.com, September 3, 2007, http://www.arabianbusiness .com/499054-china-gcc-investment-set-to-surge.

65. *Direction of Trade Statistics Quarterly December 2007*, 96–97.

66. Xiao Yu and Damien Ryan, "Citic to Construct Smelter in Egypt," *International Herald Tribune*, September 12, 2006, http://www.iht.com/articles/2006/09/11/bloomberg/bxcitic.php.

67. Shakir Husain, "Aluminum Extrusion Rides Region's Construction Boom," *Gulf News*, February 20, 2008, http://www.gulfnews.com/business/Construction/10190986.html.

68. Associated Press, "China Inks Energy Deals with Saudis," April 24, 2006, http://www.taipeitimes.com/News/world/archives/2006/04/24/2003304288.

69. "Sinopec to Set up JV with SABIC," Sina.com, February 1, 2008, http://www.china.org.cn/english/business/241713.htm.

70. Embassy of the People's Republic of China in Libyan Arab Jamahiriya, "The Economic Cooperation between China and Libya," February 12, 2007, http://ly.china-embassy.org/eng/jmgx/t297043.htm.

71. "Chinese Chemicals Giant Launches Middle East Expansion in Egypt," ExpansionManagement.com, January 5, 2007, http://www.expansionmanagement.com/cmd/articledetail/articleid/18256/default.asp.

72. Thomas Lum and Dick Nanto, "China's Trade with the United States and the World," Congressional Research Service, January 4, 2007, http://www.fas.org/sgp/crs/row/RL31403.pdf.

73. World Trade Organization, "Technical Notes—International Trade Statistics," http://www.wto.org/english/res_e/statis_e/its2003_e/technotes_e.htm.

74. "Middle East Next Hot Export Market for China Manufacturers—Global Sources Survey," Global Sources' China Supplier Survey, June 4, 2007, http://www.prnewswire.com/cgi-bin/stories.pl?ACCT=104&STORY=/www/story/06-04-2007/0004600622&EDATE=.

75. "What to Do in Dubai: Dubai Dragon Mart," Dubaicity, http://www.dubaicity.com/what_to_do_in_dubai/dubai_dragon_mart.htm.

76. U.S. Census Bureau, "Foreign Trade Statistics," www.census.gov/foreign-trade/balance/c5700.html.

77. Ibid.

78. Michael Moore, "The US-UAE Trade and Investment Relationship," US-UAE Business Council, January 2008, http://www.usuaebusiness.org/view/resources/uploaded/USUAE_Business_Counci_%20White_Paper_14Jan08.pdf.

79. Economist Intelligence Unit, "Near East Meets Far East: The Rise of Gulf Investment in Asia," October 2007.

80. Eric Dash, "Citigroup to Sell $7.5 Billion Stake to Abu Dhabi," New York Times, November 27, 2007, http://www.nytimes.com/2007/11/27/business/27citi-web.html?scp=1&sq=abu+dhabi+citigroup+&st=nyt.

81. "Merrill Lynch Enhances Its Capital Position with Agreement to Issue $6.6 Billion in Preferred Stock to Long-Term Investors," Merrill Lynch, January 15, 2008, http://www.ml.com/index.asp?id=7695_7696_8149_88278_88282_88849.

82. Economist Intelligence Unit, "Near East Meets Far East."

83. "Kuwait to Buy Large Stake in IPO of Chinese Bank," International

Herald Tribune, September 25, 2006, http://www.iht.com/articles/2006/09/24/business/hot.php.

84. Kuwait Investment Authority, "Kuwait Investment Authority Is a Cornerstone Investor in Industrial and Commercial Bank of China," http://www.kia.gov.kw/KIA/Press+Room/Press+Releases/EN/PressRelease.htm.

85. Reuters, "ICBC Says to Set up First Gulf branch in Qatar," February 1, 2008, http://www.reuters.com/article/fundsFundsNews/idUSPEK18526420080201.

86. Will Hadfield, "Chinese Manufacturer Opens Jordan's First Car Plant," *Middle East Economic Digest*, February 4, 2008, http://www.meed.com/news/2008/02/chinese_manufacturer_opens_jordans_first_car_plant.html.

87. "Jordan to Establish First Car Assembly Plant." *MENA Report*, February 4, 2008, http://www.menareport.com/en/business/221834.

88. Embassy of the People's Republic of China in the Arab Republic of Egypt, "China Invests $16m for Textile Makeover in Egypt," November 21, 2005, http://eg.china-embassy.org/eng/dsxx/t223560.htm. See also Embassy of India in Cairo, "Embassy of India, Cairo: Economic and Commercial Report for the Month of November 2005," November 2005, http://www.tradeindia.com/newsletters/country_focus/country_focus_3_jan_2006_cairo.html.

89. Xiao Yu and Damien Ryan, "Citic to Construct Smelter in Egypt." See also "China and Egypt Go Hand in Hand," *Jane's Islamic Affairs*, January 18, 2007, http://www.janes.com/security/international_security/news/jiaa/jiaa070118_1_n.shtml.

90. Soraya Permatasari and Theresa Tang, "MMC and Chalco plan Saudi aluminum plant," *International Herald Tribune*, October 4, 2007, http://www.iht.com/articles/2007/10/04/business/sxmmc.php.

91. "Chinese Chemicals Giant Launches Middle East Expansion."

92. Abdulaziz Sager , "Saudi-Chinese Relations: Energy first, but Not Last," *Arab News*, January 23, 2006, http://www.arabnews.com/?page=7&section=0&article=76692&d=23&m=1&y=2006.

93. Consulate General of the People's Republic of China in San Francisco, "Foreign Ministry Spokesperson Jiang Yu's Regular Press Conference on January 22, 2008," January 22, 2008, http://www.chinaconsulatesf.org/eng/xw/fyrth/t402395.htm.

94. BBC News, "Arafat Asks Jiang to Appoint Envoy," April 15, 2000, http://news.bbc.co.uk/2/hi/middle_east/714796.stm.

95. For an early signal of Chinese ambitions, see United Nations, "Transcript of Press Conference by Secretary-General Kofi Annan at United Nations Headquarters, January 14, 2003," January 14, 2003, http://domino.un.org/

UNISPAL.NSF/85255db800470aa485255d8b004e349a/ddc83d6725ded9b28
5256cae00674fb6!OpenDocument.

96. BBC News, "China Ups Lebanon Force to 1,000," September 18, 2006, http://news.bbc.co.uk/2/hi/asia-pacific/5355128.stm.

97. Dingli Shen, "Iran's Nuclear Ambitions Test China's Wisdom," *The Washington Quarterly* (Spring 2006), 55–66, http://www.twq.com/06spring/docs/06spring_shen.pdf.

98. Warren Hoge, "Security Council Is Stalled over Iran's Nuclear Program," *New York Times*, March 22, 2006, http://www.nytimes.com/2006/03/22/international/middleeast/22iran.html?_r=1&pagewanted=print&oref=slogin).

99. Francois Heisbourg, *Iran, Le Choix des Armes* (Geneva: Editions Stock, 2007), 38–39.

100. Shibley Telhami, "Anwar Sadat Chair for Peace and Development University of Maryland/ Zogby International 2006 Annual Arab Public Opinion Survey," Saban Center for Middle East Policy at the Brookings Institution, February 8, 2007, http://www.brookings.edu/views/speeches/telhami20070208 .pdf.

101. Ellen Knickmeyer, "Strictures in U.S. Prompt Arabs to Study Elsewhere," *Washington Post*, December 20, 2007, http://www.washingtonpost .com/wp-dyn/content/article/2007/12/19/AR2007121902501.html. See also "New Zealand Universities Attract over 300 Saudi Arabian Students," February 7, 2007, http://www.workpermit.com/news/2007_02_07/new_zealand/ saudi_arabia_scholarship_university.htm.

102. BBC News, "U.S. Lawmakers Criticize Ports Deal," February 21, 2006, http://news.bbc.co.uk/2/hi/americas/4734728.stm.

103. Telhami, "2006 Annual Arab Public Opinion Survey."

104. Naguib Mahfouz, "China for Us," *Al-Ahram*, January 31, 2002, http:// weekly.ahram.org.eg/2002/571/op6.htm.

105. Mohammad Ben Hwidan, "Al Arab wal-Namudhaj al-Sini" [Arabs and the Chinese example], *al-Bayan,* March 6, 2008, http://www.albayan.ae/ servlet/Satellite?c=Article&cid=1201709073896&pagename=Albayan%2FAr ticle%2FPrint&sType=print.

106. Abdel-Moneim Said, "Shared Past, Different Futures," *Al-Ahram*, August 18, 2005, http://weekly.ahram.org.eg/2005/756/op3.htm.

107. Tu Longde, "Chinese Craze' Rising along the Nile," China Radio International, October 12, 2004, http://english.hanban.edu.cn/market/HanBanE/ 412128.htm.

108. "Chinese Studies Available in Egypt's Top University," *People's Daily*,

October 10, 2004, http://english.peopledaily.com.cn/200410/10/eng20041010 _159608.html.

109. China Education and Research Network, "China, Egypt Sign Agreement on Establishing Chinese University," April 27, 2005, http://www.edu.cn/ Internationaledu_1499/20060323/t20060323_124312.shtml.

110. Economist Intelligence Unit, "Near East Meets Far East: The Rise of Gulf Investment in Asia."

111. Roula Khalaf, Richard McGregor, and Sundeep Tucker, "The Great Bridge of China: How Energy-hungry Beijing Hews Its Mideast Links," *Financial Times*, February 12 2007, http://www.ft.com/cms/s/0/582bb7ae-ba3d-11db -89c8-0000779e2340.html.

112. "Chinese Tourists Welcomed in Foreign Countries," *People's Daily*, February 15, 2008, http://english.people.com.cn/90001/90782/92900/6354887.html.

113. Rehab Saad, "Shifting Tourist Sands," *Al-Ahram*, January 10, 2006, http://weekly.ahram.org.eg/2006/777/eg3.htm.

114. "Chinese Ambassador Welcomes First Group of Chinese Tourists to Egypt," *People's Daily*, May 6, 2002, http://english.peopledaily.com.cn/200205/ 06/eng20020506_95200.shtml. See also "Interview: Egypt Welcomes More Chinese Tourists," *People's Daily*, October 20, 2006, http://english.peopledaily.com .cn/200610/20/eng20061020_313829.html.

115. Lu Haoting, "Arabian Flights," *China Daily*, December 31, 2007, http:// www.chinadaily.com.cn/bw/2007-12/31/content_6360999.htm. See also "Emirates Set to Serve Dubai-Shanghai Route Twice Daily," August 26, 2007, http:// www.travelscoop.co.nz/emirates-set-to-serve-dubai-shanghai-route-twice -daily/.

CHAPTER FOUR

THE UNITED STATES

The Middle East has been a central focus of U.S. strategy for six decades. The United States moved into the region in the aftermath of World War II, when Britain began pulling up its roots in the Levant, and moved in further after Britain pulled out of the Gulf in 1971. As suggested earlier, the special relationship between the United States and Saudi Arabia began under President Roosevelt, and President Johnson forged a close partnership with Israel that has grown progressively closer since. For four decades, the U.S. position in the Middle East sought to block Soviet influence, and for the last decade or so, the United States has sought to limit the influence of radical Islam. Something important happened over the last half century: the United States government accustomed itself to the prevailing order of the Middle East and committed itself to its preservation.

In recent years, China's rising influence in the Middle East has raised U.S. sensitivities. Several times in the last decade, Chinese military sales, sharing of Israeli military technology, and economic cooperation with countries such as Iran have raised U.S. ire. More broadly, skeptics of China's intentions see the country as a new spoiler for U.S. interests, competing for the affection of the region's leaders and coddling rogue regimes. U.S. diplomatic strategy in the Middle East seeks to unify the international community behind isolating some governments and rewarding others, but China's often-independent assessment of its interests and the means to achieve them threatens that effort.

Although Chinese actions in the Middle East represent Chinese assessments of their own self-interest, some in the United States see China's actions undermining U.S. influence and threatening U.S. long-term interests. The two countries are not on a collision course, but the Middle East could emerge as a key irritant in bilateral relations, and rivalry in the region would undermine each's interests and detract from regional security as well.

THE U.S. COMMITMENT TO THE MIDDLE EAST

Although the United States has had a historic commitment to protect Western Europe and a long history of projecting power in the Pacific, the Middle East has been a rising concern for the United States over the last half century. From basing Marines in Beirut in 1982 to reflagging Kuwaiti tankers in 1987 to major military operations against Iraq in 1991 and 2003, the operational tempo in the Middle East has been steadily increasing for U.S. troops. Staffing has increased commensurately. The U.S. Central Command's (CENTCOM) base in Florida houses approximately 6,000 soldiers and civilians, a number higher than the State Department's entire Washington presence, and tens of thousands of U.S. troops are based in the Persian Gulf outside of the Iraqi theater of operations. Even absent current military operations in Iraq and Afghanistan, U.S. military spending in the region is high. Some scholars suggest that from 1980 to 1990, the United States spent approximately $33 billion a year defending Middle Eastern oil supplies, and an analyst suggests that the figure for 2003 ranged between $37 billion and $44 billion.[1]

At the same time, the United States has invested tens of billions of dollars in its diplomatic position in the Middle East, most notably into efforts to resolve—or at least manage—the Arab-Israeli conflict. The United States has given Israel and Egypt together approximately $5 billion a year for three decades in the aftermath of their 1979 peace treaty, and it has heaped additional aid on Jordan in reward for its own peace agreement with Israel. Major diplomatic efforts to resolve the conflict—from 1973 to 1975, 1991 to 1992, and 1993 to 2000—have directly engaged the highest levels of the U.S. government for sustained periods of time, not only helping structure the entire U.S. approach to the Middle East, but also creating a vital priority for U.S. diplomacy globally.

U.S. PROBLEMS WITH CHINA'S INVOLVEMENT
IN THE MIDDLE EAST

It is into this context that China is making greater inroads into the Middle East, principally in terms of seeking access to its oil and gas reserves (figure 4.1).

It is a fear for energy security—rather than a concern over energy adequacy itself—that could fuel Sino-American tensions in the Middle East. Some U.S. analysts fear that a Chinese military buildup, especially the prospect of blue-water navy and power-projection capabilities, could challenge U.S. control of vital sea-lanes. Analysts wonder about the purpose of the Chinese-built deep-sea port in Gwadar, Pakistan, and its implications for a Chinese military presence far beyond the Pacific Ocean. Gwadar is only 45 miles from the Iranian border and 250 miles from the Strait of Hormuz, making it close to the region's most vital waterways. In addition to three ship berths, China has invested in a highway from Gwadar to Karachi, another Pakistani port city. Still, such an eventuality is just barely on the horizon; the Chinese possessed no aircraft carriers at the beginning of 2007, and their capacity to regulate and dominate the 7,000 miles of ocean between Shanghai and the Strait of Hormuz lies, by generous estimate, half a century down the road.[2] In addition, at present, the Chinese have expressed satisfaction with simply "free-riding" off of U.S. control of the aforementioned supply lines.[3] Still, many in the U.S. policy community express deep concern.

U.S. CONCERNS WITH CHINESE MILITARY CAPABILITIES

Despite the pressing U.S. need to engage China on questions of economic and environmental sustainability generally, and energy security specifically, U.S. concerns with the prospect of "China's rise" have instead focused disproportionately on military capabilities. A July 2006 Congressional Research Service report entitled "Sino-U.S. Relations: Current Issues and Implications for U.S. Policy," for example, devoted little more than a paragraph to Sino-U.S. energy competition in the Middle East in a 38-page report.[4] Many in the United States tend to accuse China of vastly understating its military capabilities, and China likewise accuses the United States of vastly overstating them. The danger for the United States lies not in attempting to account for all possibilities—any rational government must do this—but rather in allowing

Figure 4.1. World Proved Crude Oil Reserves, 2008 Estimates

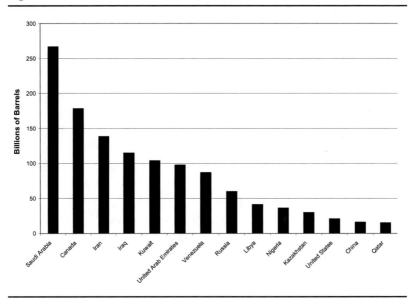

Source: U.S. Energy Information Administration, "World Proved Crude Oil Reserves, January 1, 1980–January 1, 2008 Estimates," available at http://www.eia.doe.gov/pub/international/iealf/crudeoilreserves.xls.

such calculus to determine the parameters of the broader policy debate over China, obscuring the myriad opportunities for cooperation that still exist.

Those paying attention to China's military development in recent years essentially fall into two categories: those whose role is to anticipate worst-case scenarios—in other words, what China *could* do—and those seeking to understand what China probably *will* do (the classic distinction between capabilities and intentions). The U.S. defense and intelligence communities, as well as certain congressional organizations, fall into the former category. The U.S. Department of Defense's *Quadrennial Defense Report 2006* (QDR2006) voiced the concerns of this group most succinctly: "Of the major and emerging powers, China has the greatest potential to compete militarily with the United States and field disruptive military technologies that could over time off set traditional U.S. military advantages absent U.S. counter-strategies."[5]

In the "intentions" group fall various think-tank and media analysts who can afford to take a broader view of the question of Chinese military capabilities. For example, the International Institute of Strategic Studies' *Military Balance 2007* regards China's 2006 defense white paper and the subsequent U.S. response as in keeping with the typical back-and-forth of Sino-U.S. rhetoric on military issues, rather than as a cause for alarm.[6] For the time being, lack of transparency on both sides with regard to military capabilities poses a bigger immediate problem than actual comparative capabilities, because it can have an inflammatory effect on Sino-U.S. relations. Furthermore, there must be a greater recognition that increased military capability does not necessarily imply greater aggressive intention. In this analysis, China is building itself up because it feels weak, not because it feels strong.

SUPPORTING U.S. ENEMIES

U.S. and Chinese officials have increasingly sparred regarding China's relationships with Middle Eastern governments hostile to the United States. Whereas the Chinese appear to view their efforts as one of maintaining cooperative relations with all countries in the Middle East, the United States views such efforts as undermining international efforts to isolate troubling regimes and thus compel a change in their behavior (see this volume's chapter 2 for a fuller description of the Chinese view).

One of the greatest areas of strategic difference is with policy toward Iran.[7] Despite ending its support for the Iranian nuclear program in 1997 and outwardly backing the UN's nonproliferation efforts, China has been supplying conventional arms to Iran since the mid-1980s and continues to do so today. During the Iran-Iraq War, it sold various anti-ship missiles to the Islamic Republic, including HY-2s (often referred to as the Silkworm), C-801s, and C-802s. China's weapons relationship with Iran has taken on a new strategic significance since China became a net oil importer in 1993. Weapons transfers became part of the process of mutually beneficial exchange whereby China could secure energy deals with Iran. U.S. military planners fear that Chinese anti-ship missiles could help Iran resist U.S. military efforts if conflict broke out in the Straits of Hormuz.[8] One such anti-ship missile, a likely Iranian clone of the Chinese-made C-802, was fired by Hezbollah forces during the Lebanon war of 2006, hitting an Israeli Saar 5 class ship off the coast of Lebanon. The attack killed four Israeli crewmen and did significant damage to the ship, including destroying its helicopter pad. Iran has reportedly produced its own version based on the Chinese model referred to as Noor.[9]

The United States also considers blocking any Iranian nuclear weapons capability a vital U.S. interest. Although Iran denies seeking such capabilities and China professes a similar desire to block Iranian acquisition of nuclear weapons, differences between China and the United States over nonproliferation diplomacy are an increasing irritant in the relationship. Chinese representatives profess fear that the United States is not motivated by nonproliferation concerns, but rather by aspirations of regime change. They see such a move undermining peace and stability in the Gulf rather than strengthening it. Meanwhile, U.S. critics of China's actions see China's desire as undermining U.S. efforts at diplomacy, making favorable deals for Iranian oil while relying on the United States to contain the fallout of any successful Iranian proliferation effort (or, perhaps, encouraging such a development so as to constrain U.S. influence in the Gulf). To date, China has remained a part of the P5+1 diplomatic efforts, joining international efforts to pressure Iran to suspend uranium enrichment and plutonium reprocessing and production. As Chinese (and Arab) fears grow that the U.S. intends to use an international process only to set up a more unilateral action meant to depose the current Iranian regime, China is increasingly likely to emerge as an obstacle to such a process, potentially exacerbating tensions with the United States. So far, China has been careful not to be too antagonistic, and although it held up the Security Council vote in 2006 along with Russia, China voted yes at the last three Security Council resolution votes: 1696 (2006), 1737 (2006) and 1747 (2007), all dealing with Iran's nuclear program.[10] With China's veto power as a permanent member, however, U.S. concerns over China's ability to disrupt its intentions will continue.

ATTRACTING U.S. ALLIES

In recent years, the combination of long-held grievances and more recent objections to U.S. foreign policy in the Middle East has encouraged certain states, even those that are traditionally U.S. allies, to seek a greater degree of distance from the United States. Egypt and Saudi Arabia, for example, often appear eager to diversify their economic and diplomatic relations as part of their broader desire to balance the uncontested influence of the United States in the Middle East. These tendencies have grown as the assertive policies of the Bush administration have roused anti-American sentiment and fear of instability among Middle Eastern publics. Some of these countries see in China a beneficial business partner, a growing consumer market, and an attractive venue for investment; others see a source of diplomatic support. China is more attractive than the United States to many because it does not impose conditions on its aid and trade and because it lacks the West's unfavorable history and image in the Middle East. Chinese diplomats profess to be guided by principle rather than interests or the ability to coerce opponents, drawing a distinction in the popular mind between U.S. and Chinese behavior.

Israel too has had a long-standing and rather unique relationship with China, with the former providing much of the Western technology that China has required for its military modernization. In fact, some suggest that Israel remains China's second-largest supplier of weaponry after Russia.[11] These weapons were primarily used to build up China's capabilities and edge in the Taiwan Strait. The Sino-Israeli relationship was a significant source of tension between Israel and the United States in the 1990s, with Israel's proposed sale of Phalcon (Airborne Early Warning, Command and Control) aircraft to China and again with Israel's agreement to upgrade China's Harpy armed drones in 2004 (see this volume's chapter 3 for a more detailed analysis of these episodes).[12] Those incidents led to an Israeli agreement in 2005 to limit sensitive military sales to China and notify the United States before any such sales. After that point, technology transfers appear to have returned to levels deemed acceptable by the U.S. defense and intelligence communities. Israel's primary motivations in its relationship with China are financial, though some also believe that Israel seeks to cultivate independent arms relations with China as a means of encouraging Beijing not to sell certain weapons to Israel's enemies.[13] Much like China's arms relations with other Middle Eastern states, the Israel relationship is probably not sufficient to cause a more general conflict between China and the United States, though it is in U.S. interests to pursue cooperation with China in areas like energy security in order to ensure that China's relations with Middle Eastern states have a stabilizing rather than destabilizing effect.

BROADER AMERICAN THINKING ABOUT CHINA

Narrow differences of view regarding China's actions in the Middle East fit into broader U.S. debates about China's future on the global stage. Although some engage in a mostly intellectual exercise as they seek to understand the trajectory of China's "rise," many others foresee a practical "power shift" to Asia, in which China supplants the United States as the global superpower. The phrase "peaceful rise"—popular among Chinese themselves—communicates instead the notion of China's coming to power alongside the United States and other members of the international community.[14]

Some academic debates contain a more explicit policy element, as the U.S. response to China's transformation has become in recent years a fascinating case study for those who study different theories of international relations and who attempt to predict what the future of the Sino-U.S. relationship will look like.[15] Some, such as G. John Ikenberry, argue that China's growing power can be "managed." These thinkers advocate a "milieu-based approach" to U.S. grand strategy in the coming years, in which the United States "places itself at the center of a series of new global institutions where nations could come together and solve common problems."[16]

In contrast, those who subscribe to the realist school argue that China's growing power must be contained—because nation-states will continue to be the basic unit of international relations well into the twenty-first century, and leaders will continue to think along basically national, zero-sum lines. Robert Kagan has criticized internationalists such as Ikenberry, asking "Which China is it? A twenty-first century power that wants to be integrated into a liberal international order, which would mean both a transformation of its own polity and a limitation of its strategic ambitions? Or a nineteenth-century power that wants to preserve its rule at home and expand its reach abroad?"[17]

Although the internationalist school provides a desirable framework to work toward, it does not sufficiently respond to the realist critique. The realist school, on the other hand, threatens to give birth to a self-fulfilling prophecy whereby the United States conducts policy as though China were an enemy, and in so doing gradually offends China enough to make it actually an enemy. In the words of *New York Times* columnist David Brooks, the problem is that "we're trapped in a hybrid world, in which many problems are postnational but the social structures are unavoidably national."[18]

Similar division and confusion characterizes popular debates about China in the United States as well. A 2006 study by World Public Opinion found that in February 2006, 47 percent of American respondents said that the prospect of China's emergence as a world power poses a threat to the United States. About China's economic growth specifically, Americans polled were split evenly over whether it constituted a "negative" or a "positive" for the United States. Those polled were similarly divided almost half and half over the question of whether China presents a military threat to the United States. The only question about which American respondents were fairly certain was the prospect of China's becoming as militarily powerful as the United States: three-quarters saw such an eventuality as a negative, whereas only 59 percent of respondents in the rest of the 22 nations polled agreed.[19] One might argue that Americans' generally equivocal and divided stance toward China, mirroring the dichotomy in academic debates, is a symptom of the U.S. lack of a comprehensive policy toward China globally, let alone in the Middle East.

China's economic weight has made it the second-largest U.S. trading partner after Canada, accounting for 12 percent of total trade (figures 4.2 and 4.3).[20] The greater economic interdependence has also made Americans wary. Fears of China reverberate among both citizens and Congress. There is an urge among U.S. lawmakers to "get tough with Beijing."[21] Members of Congress cite China's increasing bilateral trade surplus and the increasing U.S. deficit as proof of China's unfair currency practices, illegal export subsidies, intellectual property violations, and general disregard for international trade regulations.[22] As of 2007, China owned $477.6 billion in U.S. treasury securities, making it the second-largest foreign holder after Japan and comprising nearly 20 percent of all foreign ownership.[23]

Dozens of legislative measures have been proposed, mostly dealing with China's trade practices. In July 2005, the House passed H.R. 3283 to apply U.S. countervailing duties against subsidized imports from China and other "nonmarket economies."[24] In November of that same year, Congress intervened directly in H.R. 3058 (signed by President Bush on November 30) to prohibit the Department of Treasury from approving the sale of Unocal to the Chinese National Offshore Oil Corporation, or CNOOC, which had made a $18.5 billion bid for the American oil company.[25] Finally, Senator Schumer introduced during the 109th Congress a bill (S. 295) that proposed a 27.5 percent ad valorem increase in U.S. import tariffs on Chinese goods, a measure that won substantial bipartisan support despite its potentially disastrous economic implications; the bill remains unresolved as of August 2007.[26]

Figure 4.2. Top Five U.S. Trade Partners (Total Trade, 2007)

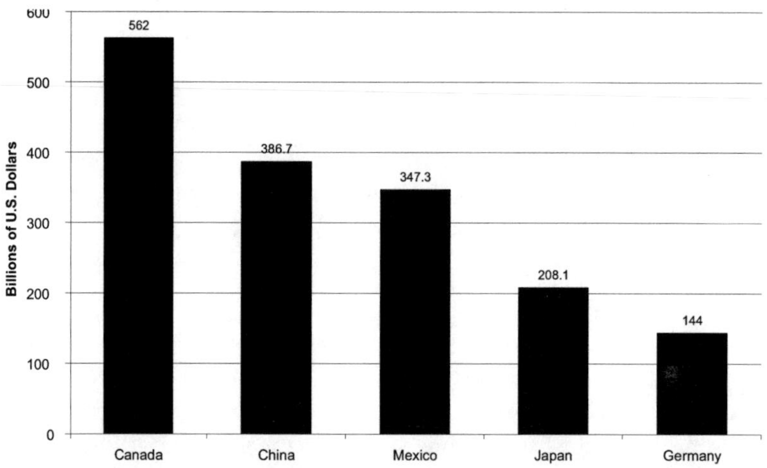

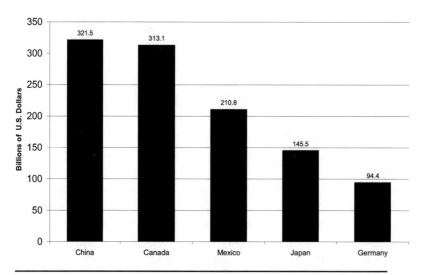

Source: U.S. Census Bureau, "Top Trading Partners—Total Trade, Exports, Imports," available at http://www.census.gov/foreign-trade/statistics/highlights/top/top0712.html.

Figure 4.3. Top Five U.S. Trade Partners (U.S. Imports, 2007)

Source: U.S. Census Bureau, "Top Trading Partners—Total Trade, Exports, Imports," available at http://www.census.gov/foreign-trade/statistics/highlights/top/top0712.html.

More broadly, China for Americans has become a scapegoat for many domestic socioeconomic concerns. China, with its relative disregard for human rights and its affinity for ruthless cost cutting, has labor costs with which most countries simply cannot compete. Thus China has become the target of resentment for many outsourced American jobs, along with a host of other discontents whose true source lies within the United States. Politicians find it too easy to mobilize this resentment and too difficult to address these discontents—let alone the broader strategic issues at stake. In the words of Rep. Duncan Hunter (R-Calif.), China is "cheating on trade and they're buying ships, planes, and missiles with our money, as well as taking millions of jobs."[27] According to a Democratic political analyst, especially in anticipation of the 2008 election year, politicians are adopting an "economic populism that reflects the overall anxiety the American people have over the economy and that their children's future is being traded and sold to countries like China."[28]

At the same time, popular anxiety about the Middle East is increasing in the United States. Still reeling from the events of September 11, Americans increasingly see the Middle East as an area full of menacing threats. According to a September 2007 poll in the United States, 40 percent ranked the Middle East as the country's biggest foreign policy problem, more than twice the second-leading problem.[29] Overlapping crises in Iraq and Iran, the enduring threat of terrorism, and the persistence of extremism throughout the region have many Americans convinced that the stakes in the Middle East are remarkably high. Americans sometimes see Chinese actions in the region, however minor, not merely as complicating U.S. policy, but by extension increasing the threats that Americans face.

Concern with Chinese actions in the Middle East mirrors broader U.S. concerns about the country. Most candidates in the 2008 presidential campaign have made China a significant issue, though certainly not a top-priority one. At best, candidates' statements have realistically but vaguely asserted that China is both a competitor and a partner: both writing in the July/August 2007 issue of *Foreign Affairs*, Barack Obama and Mitt Romney articulated slightly different versions of this position.[30] At worst, candidates have refused to even provide that degree of specificity, basing their preliminary policy recommendations around the same fears that plague Congress: Hillary Clinton, despite superior understanding of the issue of Chinese holdings of

U.S. public debt, appears reluctant to espouse any particular position as of yet. According to one political analyst, Clinton is a particularly vulnerable candidate on the China issue because she once served on the board of directors of Wal-Mart—which has been accused of extensive outsourcing to China—and because her husband was largely responsible for persuading Congress in 2000 to grant China permanent normal trade relations status and for facilitating China's acceptance to the World Trade Organization.[31] Even outside of politicized, spur-of-the-moment debate, when given the opportunity for nuanced analysis, candidates have found it easier to return inevitably to U.S. fears of China rather than moving toward suggestions for responsible policy. For example, in a speech to the Hoover Institution, John McCain stated that

> China . . . [has] joined Russia in hindering international efforts to put pressure on dictators in Iran, Sudan, Zimbabwe, Burma, and other pariah states. China expresses its desire for a stable peace in East Asia, but it continues to increase its military might, fostering distrust and concerns in the region about Beijing's ambitions. We must insist that China use its newfound power responsibly at home and abroad.[32]

In other words, most candidates have not moved significantly beyond stating that the United States needs a China strategy.

The politics and rhetoric of presidential candidates is only a barometer of the broader disconnects and indecision that characterize perceptions of and approaches toward China in the U.S. policymaking community. Of course, it is true that the U.S. government has set up some potentially fruitful cooperative institutions. The best examples of this are the State Department's U.S.-China Senior Dialogue and the Treasury Department's Strategic Economic Dialogue (SED), both of which derived from meetings between U.S. President George W. Bush and Chinese President Hu Jintao in 2005–2006.[33] The basic objectives of these two institutions overlap considerably. That said, the Senior Dialogue focuses on resolving and averting conflicts in the short term, whereas the SED focuses on isolating common strategic interests and opportunities for cooperation in the long term. The first Senior Dialogue aimed to cover "trade and economic issues, energy security, increasing cooperation against terrorism, issues of democracy, and human rights."[34] This first meeting immediately preceded the famous fall 2005 remarks by Deputy Secretary of State Robert Zoellick (who cochaired the first two dialogues) that China must become a "responsible stakeholder" in the international community. The SED, on the other hand, aims to "ensure that the benefits of our growing economic relationship with China are fairly shared by citizens of both countries," covering many of the same issues as the Senior Dialogue, but concentrating more on the rules of the game than on the game itself. In the broadest sense, however, both dialogues can be said from a U.S. perspective to promote cooperation with China based on the "responsible stakeholder" idea. These two dialogues build on and further encourage China's involvement—or, what the United States calls its "successful integration"—in the UN Security Council, the World Trade Organization, and the Asia-Pacific Economic Cooperation (APEC) forum. Even if concrete results do not emerge from every meeting of these two dialogues, their mere existence certainly provides a useful framework that can diffuse potential conflicts and emphasize opportunities for cooperation.

Progress made by the Senior Dialogue and SED notwithstanding, a definite rhetorical and methodological disconnect exists between the Departments of Treasury and State and the Department of Defense. In particular, the annual release of the DOD's *Military Power of the People's Republic of China* tends to take a more skeptical view of China. For example, the 2007 report stated in its Executive Summary that

> The outside world has limited knowledge of the motivations, decision-making, and key capabilities supporting China's military modernization. China's leaders have yet to explain adequately the purposes or desired endstates of the PLA's expanding military capabilities. China's actions in certain areas increasingly appear inconsistent with its declaratory policies. Actual Chinese defense expenditures remain far above officially disclosed figures. This lack of transparency in China's military affairs will naturally and understandably prompt international responses that hedge against the unknown.[35]

This same sort of skepticism appears to apply not only to Chinese assessments of U.S. actions and intentions in the Middle East, but also of Arab ones. In both Chinese and the Arab views, the uncontested hegemony of the United States essentially began with collapse of the USSR and the first invasion of Iraq in 1990.

The good news for the United States, at the moment, is that China remains unlikely to succumb to the temptation of challenging U.S.

hegemony in the region in any large way. There are a material and conceptual explanations for this. The material explanation is that while China is putting people on the ground in the Middle East, they have not yet tied up significant amounts of investment capital in the region. The conceptual explanation is that the Chinese and Middle Easterners still have quite different visions regarding China's role in the Middle East and in the world. Whereas many in the Middle East wish China to emerge as an alternative pole to U.S. influence—some to blunt U.S. power and others to force the U.S. to compete for their affections—China seems to have no appetite for such a gambit, seeking positive relations with all. Although Chinese policymakers may believe that the United States is acting as a hegemon in the Middle East, they evince little intention of creating a head-on rivalry.

Still, U.S. policymakers ought to take more careful note of how Arab and Chinese views of the United States are aligning. This process has formed a basis for mutual understanding between China and many Middle Easterners, which in turn facilitates relationships beneficial to both parties. Meanwhile, the United States has not reached a consensus on what its approach to China should be, let alone its approach to China's Middle East policy.

NONMILITARY COMPETITION

Military conflict between the United States and China is extremely unlikely in the foreseeable future, as the reasons for peaceful relations are simply too heavily weighted against such a possibility. Among them are a bilateral trade relationship currently worth more than $300 billion annually, the risk of the United States using its naval supremacy to cut off Chinese oil imports and thus dealing a grievous blow to its development drive, and the fact that such action would drastically diminish both nations' international legitimacy for years to come.

That China will not directly challenge the United States, however, does not mean that it doubts the likelihood of its eventually inheriting global predominance. Indeed, it may reflect instead the Chinese effort to learn from the lessons of history: when Athens challenged Sparta, when Carthage challenged Rome, when Napoleon challenged Europe, when Germany challenged the Allies, and when the Soviet Union challenged the United States, the ascending and prematurely aggressive power was consistently and decisively shown its place by the dominant one. In fact, the only recent example of a successful great-power transition in recent world history, in China's eyes, occurred as the United States "took over" for Britain's predominance in world affairs—very gradually and almost entirely peacefully—from the mid-eighteenth to the mid-twentieth centuries. Thus, it may be that China refuses to challenge the United States precisely because it seeks to one day replace it.

That said, actual U.S. conflict with China in the Middle East has been quite limited, but there is a definite sense that conflict might become significantly more acute in the future if energy security and other aspects of the Sino-U.S. relationship are not responsibly managed. On top of this, events in the Middle East itself carry the potential to alter the strategic landscape in a way that would encourage greater Sino-U.S. competition—a reality that must be viewed in large part as the result of U.S. policy in the region.

SINO-U.S. ECONOMIC COMPETITION IN THE MIDDLE EAST

Direct Competition

Both the United States and China have their respective traditional allies in the Middle East when it comes to economic (and other) relationships. The United States tends to support and trade with Egypt, Israel, Jordan, Kuwait, and the United Arab Emirates, whereas China has cultivated relationships with Iran, Syria, Iraq, Algeria, and Oman; only Saudi Arabia has been able to develop a balanced relationship with both powers, largely due to its decisive role in global oil markets.

One of the only major cases of Sino-U.S. economic competition with Middle East implications was the $18.5 billion bid by CNOOC in 2005 to acquire Unocal, a California-based American oil company with pipeline interests extending into the Middle East. This, the largest foreign takeover attempt ever by a Chinese firm, ultimately drew insurmountable political opposition from Congress. As for Unocal, it snubbed CNOOC's offer and eventually accepted a significantly lower offer from Chevron. On the one hand, the fact that CNOOC is partially state-owned seemed to many to indicate that the bid was merely part of a larger picture, whereby the Chinese government itself sought to demonstrate a new aggressiveness vis-à-vis the United States. Furthermore, it also seemed to illustrate the growing concerns over Sino-U.S. competition for global energy resources, which many concluded would sooner or later bring the two powers into a Middle

East confrontation. Such fears were substantiated by the statistic that $63 billion in mergers and acquisitions had already been announced in the oil and gas industry in the first half of 2005, as many as occurred total in 2004.[36]

On the other hand, however, the CNOOC-Unocal incident may just as easily be said to demonstrate China's weakness and lack of coordination as it does China's strength and aggression. There is evidence, for example, that Beijing never supported the CNOOC bid in the first place.[37] Moreover, some have argued more broadly that there exists a significant disconnect between the more traditional and ideologically driven Chinese Communist Party (CCP) and the Western-educated, more profit-driven Chinese business sector—state-owned or not. Given these arguments, the *Economist*, for one, has asserted that the most worrying aspect of the CNOOC-Unocal incident is not what it says about China, but what it says about the United States. Specifically, Washington's "anti-China hysteria" combined with a "cowardly silence" on the part of the pro-China business lobby, causing a disturbing disregard for fair play and open markets in which U.S. politicians somehow managed to cede the moral high ground to China.[38]

The principal debate over Sino-U.S. economic competition in the Middle East, however, concerns not what has passed but what may lie ahead. Trade with the Middle East by both China and the United States remains small compared with those countries' trade with other regions of the world. As many have noted, the real potential for economic competition between the United States and China in the Middle East is in the energy sector.[39]

Indirect Competition: Trade, Investment, and Market Access[40]

Chinese and U.S. competition for the Middle East is not about occupying territory or building the biggest embassy. Indeed, it is difficult to even say what constitutes an advantage in this "contest": is it more advantageous to have a greater presence in the Middle East and have a greater stake in events there, or to be more marginally involved in the region and thus more at the mercies of others' actions? This ambiguity lies at the heart of the Middle East dilemma for the United States and China alike: stronger relationships with Middle Eastern states means increased energy security, but it also means increased dependence and vulnerability to political developments. Given that such relationships are necessary—that is, that "energy independence" is impossible given the current levels of global demand—the true winner of economic competition in the Middle East is the power that can maximize its trade with the region (especially in energy resources) while minimizing its political and material involvement. Indeed, this has been China's strategy, to the degree that it has one.

As chapter 2 also suggests, China has sought to make energy deals with countries that the United States has sought to exclude from global energy markets for reasons of foreign policy. Although such a move helps meet the Chinese demand for oil, it has policy implications both for the Sino-American relationship as well as for the balance of power in the Middle East.

The depth of U.S. economic relationships with key Middle Eastern states has created a substantial inertia that will continue to prevent those states from throwing in all of their chips with China. For example, Saudi Arabia, the world's largest oil producer, has a special relationship with the United States, the world's largest oil consumer. It is estimated that the United States receives about 60 percent of Saudi foreign direct investment (FDI), which allows Saudis to help finance the large U.S. trade deficit with the Kingdom.[41] In 2006, bilateral trade volume between these two countries was nearly $40 billion. Of that, $32 billion consisted of Saudi exports, 98.3 percent of which were oil and other energy products.[42] China, in contrast, had a bilateral trade of $16 billion with Saudi Arabia in 2005, and the number reached only $20 billion in 2006.[43] But as a matter of proportion, the Sino-Saudi relationship is an important one. The United States is the world's largest economy, but China is the world's fastest-growing one. In 2005, the United States imported three times the amount of oil from Saudi Arabia than China did, but Saudi oil represented almost twice the percentage of oil imports to China than it did to the United States.[44]

There is evidence as well that U.S. consumption of Saudi oil as a share of its total consumption is actually decreasing. From 2003 to 2006, total U.S. oil imports increased from 12.26 million bbl/d to 13.7 million bbl/d, but imports from Saudi Arabia decreased from 1.77 million bbl/d to 1.46 million bbl/d during the same period. The United States has managed to curb its consumption of Saudi oil by importing more from countries such as Venezuela.[45] Chinese demand for imported oil is growing firmly, and the Saudi share of that oil is growing even faster. Saudi oil exports to China increased by more than 500 percent during the 1990s and continue to grow.[46]

China seems to be gaining more from Saudi Arabia than the size of its investment in the country would indicate. In 2004, Sinopec signed a gas exploration and production agreement with Saudi Aramco, a deal valued at $300 million. That same year, Sinopec also signed a deal with Saudi Aramco and ExxonMobil to build a refinery in Quanzhou, Fujian Province; this deal was valued at $3.5 billion, and ground was broken in July 2005. Finally, in 2006 the Chinese and Saudi governments signed an agreement to set up a 10-million-cubic-meter oil storage facility on Hainan Island.[47] Clearly, many of these deals remain in the planning stages. Although these deals are valued highly, China seems to have managed thus far not to have sunk very much money at all in Saudi Arabia itself. In contrast, one estimate put U.S. FDI in Saudi Arabia in 2003 alone at $4.2 billion, up from $3.8 billion in 2002.[48] The United States again invested $3.2 billion in Saudi Arabia in 2004 and $3.5 billion in 2005.[49] Furthermore, the Saudi Arabian General Investment Authority (SAGIA) announced in 2005 that the Kingdom is seeking funds for projects worth more than SR2.34 trillion ($624 billion) in vital sectors including petrochemicals, gas, railways, desalination, and electricity.[50] Although it is difficult to find comprehensive information on Chinese FDI in Saudi Arabia, it is safe to say that the majority of these funds will not come from China. Thus, Saudi Arabia supplies the United States with a smaller percentage of its oil demand than it does China, but sucks from it a larger amount of FDI.

SINO-U.S. MILITARY COMPETITION IN THE MIDDLE EAST

China's military technology dealings with Middle Eastern states have received much attention. These dealings began in the mid-1980s when China sold conventional arms to both the Iranians and the Iraqis during the 1980–1988 Iran-Iraq War and continued in 1988 when it sold a variety of cruise missiles to Saudi Arabia. China's purchases also caused alarm in the 1990s and early 2000s, its principal suppliers being Russia and Israel. China largely used these acquisitions to build up its forces in the Taiwan Strait, from time to time creating escalating tensions with the United States.[51] Finally, there is also the question of China's role in the spread of nuclear technologies to Iran, though China agreed to cease its support for the Iranian nuclear program in 1997, and since then has supported UN efforts to pressure Iran to conform to international nonproliferation standards.[52]

Despite the tension that many of these relationships have caused, they can only be properly contextualized by considering the United States' own arms dealings with the countries of the Middle East. The Gulf War of 1990–1991 caused a $42 billion expansion in the global arms industry.[53] Beginning in 1993, the U.S. government topped a list of states eager to sell off unused weapons from that conflict. Since then, the United States has continued to lead the world arms trade in both production and export, with worldwide deliveries in 2005 outnumbering those of the next-highest exporter (Great Britain) by a ratio of almost four to one. Furthermore, an increasing share of these weapons go to unstable regions, with 70.2 percent delivered to third-world countries. In comparison, China in 2005 sold only $900 million in arms to all parties (although a higher percent went to third-world countries than in U.S. sales).[54] The Middle East follows this general pattern: in contrast to China's sporadic and highly publicized dealings, the United States more quietly exported billions of dollars of arms to Middle Eastern states. Saudi Arabia often tops the list, receiving $16.6 billion from 1996 to 1999 and $6.3 billion from 2000 to 2003.[55] In an additional layer of irony, there is also evidence that some of these weapons have actually ended up in China and Iraq, rather than remaining in the hands of U.S. regional allies.[56]

High-profile arms deals between China and Middle Eastern states have become rarer in recent years, especially in the wake of noisy U.S. protests for the last decade over China's efforts to purchase Israeli weapons that contain U.S. technology or components (described more fully in chapter 3). Nevertheless, the U.S. defense and intelligence communities continue to express concern over China's sale of nuclear technology, ballistic missile technology, and advanced conventional weapons to U.S. enemies in the Middle East.[57] At the same time that concern over Chinese arms transfers to the Middle East has somewhat diminished, however, concerns are growing that China is "investing heavily in efforts to improve its ability to project power beyond its borders."[58] Specifically, Chinese investments in ports such as the one in Gwadar, Pakistan, and elsewhere have led some to conclude that the Chinese are seeking to eventually supplant U.S. global naval hegemony.[59] Once again, the day when they have the naval capacity to control the sea-lanes from the Straight of Hormuz to Shanghai is by most estimates at least half a century away.

Meanwhile, the United States in July 2007 announced a new arms deal with its Middle East allies to be worth approximately $63 billion over the next decade.[60]

SINO-U.S. POLITICO-IDEOLOGICAL COMPETITION IN THE MIDDLE EAST

For the time being, the area of greatest Sino-U.S. competition is neither that of economics nor that of military capabilities, but that of perceptions, politics, and ideologies. China has managed to portray itself in a positive light to both governments and publics, and the United States has an increasingly difficult time with both audiences.[61]

Easy for China to Look Good

The United States has long, deep, and often strained relationships with some Middle Eastern states. It bears the scars of more than a half century of efforts to impose both security and order in the Middle East, and it must continue to deal with the residue of anti-imperialist sentiment that existed long before the United States entered the region and with the Cold War rhetoric that was sustained for almost a half century. In contrast, China has more recent, less involved, friendly relationships with essentially *all* Middle Eastern states. This discrepancy exists partly because China is adept at managing its contradictions, a consequence of having clear (and limited) priorities and being able to act according to them. Few doubt that China's interests in the region are principally mercantile, but China's diplomacy has been sufficiently deft so as to allow the country to sell arms to antagonists on both sides of a number of disputes: Iranians and Iraqis in the 1980s, Israelis and Arabs in the 1990s, and Saudis and Iranians in the 2000s. China has been able to increase its own influence in the Middle East precisely by saying that it opposes any outside nation's having influence and become more powerful by asserting that it distrusts power.

Easy for the United States to Look Bad

Meanwhile, many in the Middle East believe that the United States has ceded the moral and diplomatic high ground to China. Especially as far as the Middle East is concerned, incidents and policies that reflect poorly on the international role of the United States open up conceptual space for the Chinese to criticize it—regardless of the equal or worse offenses occurring within China. For example, the apparent U.S. disregard for due process for Guantanamo prisoners has provoked similar criticism from both Chinese and Arab observers.[62] The Guantanamo issue was not merely a matter of rhetoric between the United States and China, furthermore, for the United States had detained five Uighurs in the prison that it had deemed terrorists. The United States then faced the difficult choice of continuing to detain the prisoners while being criticized by a country with a terrible human rights record or admit failure by releasing them back to that country, where they would probably be treated even worse than at Guantanamo. Eventually, Albania agreed to accept the five prisoners, but the damage had already been done.[63]

The general impasse in the Arab-Israeli peace process represents another U.S. frustration that may become an opportunity for China. The U.S. refusal to engage with Hamas and other parties not to its liking has worsened its image in Arab eyes. Israel and the Palestinian Authority have not moved to implement the Quartet's 2003 "Roadmap," and it remains unclear whether recent efforts to restart negotiations will produce concrete results.[64] In this area too China has said and done "all the right things" by multiple parties. In May 2006, Hu Jintao's government invited Hamas foreign minister Mahmoud al-Zahar to the second meeting of the Arab-Chinese Forum of Cooperation in Beijing, to the alarm of many Western observers.[65] In December of that same year, however, China also hosted a meeting of Israeli and Palestinian officials, apparently to merely agree—and all three parties certainly agreed—that China should play a larger role in the Middle East peace process. Chinese officials made it clear that it sought a greater role in order to counter the bias of "some countries."[66] Whether this represents a Chinese effort to enter the fray of Arab-Israeli negotiations or merely raise their diplomatic profile remains unclear.

The greatest damage to the U.S. reputation, however, and the greatest opportunity for the Chinese to improve their global standing at U.S. expense, has grown out of the aftermath of the U.S. invasion of Iraq. In the wake of the September 11 attacks, the United States and China looked set to embark on a new cooperative relationship to counter the spread of terrorism. The invasion of Iraq dealt a near-fatal blow to that opportunity as well as to any Arab perception that the United States could still help to provide a workable vision for the future of the Middle East. The columnist Hassan Tahsin articulated the extremely pessimistic view toward the United States toward which many Arabs then gravitated:

> In his attempt to dodge the pressures from Arab and other countries for the U.S. to pull out from Iraq, the new U.S. Defense Secretary Robert Gates spoke like Condoleezza Rice who said to her Middle Eastern audience, according to a report of the Associated Press, that the war, which has cost $350 billion in cash and the lives of 2,987 U.S. soldiers so far, is a good investment because a stable Iraq will pave the way for the birth of a new Middle East. In other words the U.S. will not hesitate to do anything to pave the way for a total U.S. presence in the region . . . . In fact, the real motive for the U.S. occupation of the Middle East is to stop the growing power of Muslims and weaken Arab countries, as well as putting an end to the increasing trend of people, particularly blacks, embracing Islam in the U.S. and Western Europe.[67]

China recognized that it stood to gain from such perceptions. For example, as in the Guantanamo case, China did not neglect the opportunity to criticize U.S. treatment of Iraqi prisoners at Abu Ghraib.[68] More broadly, China has been able to secure a position in Iraq, largely unchecked by the United States. In the summer of 2007, for instance, it renewed a 1997 oil deal with Iraq. Just as important, however, is what China has not done: by simply sitting back and remaining uninvolved, it allowed the United States to trip over itself severely in the Middle East—a region it refers to as the "graveyard of the Great Powers." The additional tangible and intangible benefits to China from the U.S. invasion of Iraq will no doubt continue to reveal themselves in the coming years.

CONCLUSION

The centrality of the Middle East in U.S. strategic thinking has not always strengthened U.S. influence in the region. In addition, being the most powerful external actor has benefits, but it also has tremendous costs on the political, military, and economic level. The United States has borne these costs, at least in part, because of its interest in maintaining an international system that broadly serves its interests. China has adeptly learned to profit from that system, especially in the Middle East, without bearing many of the costs.

There are some in the United States who would see greater Chinese engagement in the region as a challenge not only to U.S. primacy in the region, but also to U.S. interests. Their argument would be to keep the Chinese out as much as possible. Others would argue for China's playing a more responsible role in the region, which no doubt would require somewhat greater support for U.S. policy and U.S. initiatives.

For its part, China sees no particular need to shift from its current course—seeking to maximize benefits from prevailing conditions in the Middle East without seeking to change them. Some degree of U.S. difficulty in the region is to China's benefit, but a collapse of U.S. influence would certainly not be.

China's growing position in the region seems most likely to be a slight negative for the United States, making the United States compete harder for reduced gains. By contrast, the U.S. position in the Middle East is a huge win for China, as it stands to benefit from the overall stability the United States helps create while paying a only small fraction of the costs. The Middle East seems unlikely to emerge as a model for Sino-American cooperation. The elements of energy competition are just too high, and U.S. concerns about security are simply too acute. At the same time, competition in the Middle East is an unlikely spark for Sino-American conflict, in part because of overwhelming U.S. strength and in part because of the skill of Chinese policymakers in understanding the limits to which they should go.

Notes

1. David L. Greene and Paul N. Leiby, "The Oil Security Metrics Model: A Tool for Evaluating the Prospective Oil Security Benefits of DOE's Energy Efficiency and Renewable Energy R&D Programs," U.S. Department of Energy, May 2006, 23, http://pzl1.ed.ornl.gov/GreeneAndLeiby2006%20Oil%20 Security%20Metrics%20Model%20ORNL_TM_2006_505.pdf, citing U.S. General Accounting Office, *Southwest Asia: Cost of Protecting U.S. Interests*, GAO/NSIAD-91-250, Washington, D.C., August 1991, http://archive.gao.gov/d19t9/144832.pdf.

2. John Calabrese, "Dragon by the Tail," Middle East Institute, March 23, 2004, http://se1.isn.ch/serviceengine/FileContent?serviceID=PublishingHouse &fileid=5D9638C2-BB5C-6B66-36E1-776576A8A6A6&lng=en.

3. "Vital Triangle" conference summary, CSIS Middle East Program, September 2006, http://www.csis.org/media/csis/pubs/china-middle_east_summary.pdf.

4. Kerry Dumbaugh, "China-U.S. Relations: Current Issues and Implications

for U.S. Policy," Congressional Research Service, July 14, 2006, http://fas
.org/sgp/crs/row/RL32804.pdf.

5. U.S. Department of Defense, *Quadrennial Defense Review Report 2006*
(Washington, D.C.: Office of the Secretary of Defense, 2006), 29, http://www
.defenselink.mil/qdr/report/Report20060203.pdf. Similar findings are docu-
mented in U.S. Department of Defense, *Annual Report to Congress: Military
Power of the People's Republic of China, 2007* (Washington, D.C.: Office of the
Secretary of Defense, 2007); John J. Tkacik, Jr., "Panda Hedging," *Heritage
Foundation Web Memo No. 1093*, May 24, 2006, http://www.heritage.org/
research/AsiaandthePacific/wm1093.cfm; Robert D. Walpole, "The Ballistic
Missile Threat to the United States," *Central Intelligence Agency Speeches & Tes-
timony,* February 9, 2000, https://www.cia.gov/news-information/speeches-
testimony/2000/nio_speech_020900.html; and James Mulvenon and David
M. Finkelstein, eds., *China's Revolution in Doctrinal Affairs: Emerging Trends
in the Operational Art of the Chinese People's Liberation Army* (Alexandria,
Va.: CNA Corporation, 2005).

6. John Chipman, "Press Statement on *The Military Balance 2007*" (London: IISS, January 31, 2007), 4. Similar perspectives can be found in *The Economist* and in Dumbaugh, "China-U.S. Relations: Current Issues."

7. For evidence presented in the United States on China's other military ties
to the Middle East, see "Unclassified Report to Congress on the Acquisition
of Technology Relating to Weapons of Mass Destruction and Advanced Conventional Munitions, 1 July through 31 December 2003," *Central Intelligence
Agency Reports*, July–December 2003, https://www.cia.gov/library/reports/
archived-reports-1/july_dec2003.htm. Also of concern to U.S. strategists are
relations with North Korea and Pakistan. See Dumbaugh, "China-U.S. Relations: Current Issues," 19.

8. Dan Blumenthal, "Providing Arms: China and the Middle East," *Middle
East Quarterly* (Spring 2005), http://www.meforum.org/article/695. For an
extensive discussion of the Sino-Iranian military relationship, please see John
Garver, *China and Iran: Ancient Partners in a Post-Imperial World* (Seattle:
University of Washington Press, 2006), chapter 7.

9. Alon Ben-David, "Israel Navy caught out by Hizbullah hit on corvette," *Jane's
Defence Weekly*, July 26, 2006, http://www8.janes.com/Search/documentView
.do?docId=/content1/janesdata/mags/jdw/history/jdw2006/jdw24231.htm
@current&pageSelected=allJanes&keyword=iran%20hizbullah%20c-802&back
Path=http://search.janes.com/Search&Prod_Name=JDW&.

10. Warren Hoge, "Security Council Is Stalled over Iran's Nuclear Program,"
New York Times, March 22, 2006, http://www.nytimes.com/2006/03/22/
international/middleeast/22iran.html?_r=1&pagewanted=print&oref=slogin.

11. Ibid. U.S. insistence that Israel cancel recent sales to China may have caused Israel to drop significantly lower on the list of Chinese suppliers.

12. Ibid. The Phalcon deal was originally signed in 1996, but was not cancelled until 2000, when then Prime Minister Barak made the announcement at the start of the Camp David talks.

13. During the summer 2006 war in Lebanon, Hezbollah hit an Israeli warship with a Chinese-designed radar-guided missile. See Mark Mazzetti and Thom Shanker, "Arming of Hezbollah Reveals U.S. and Israeli Blind Spots," *New York Times*, July 19, 2006, http://www.nytimes.com/2006/07/19/world/middleeast/19missile.html?_r=1&oref=slogin.

14. The latter question is treated, for example, in Niall Ferguson, *The War of the World: Twentieth-Century Conflict and the Descent of the West* (New York: Penguin, 2006), and Kenneth Pomeranz, *The Great Divergence: China, Europe, and the Making of the Modern World Economy* (Princeton, N.J.: Princeton University Press, 2000), Sujian Guo, ed., *China's 'Peaceful Rise' in the 21st Century: Domestic and International Conditions* (Burlington, Vt.: Ashgate, 2006), and David Shambaugh, ed., *Power Shift: China and Asia's New Dynamics* (Berkeley: University of California Press, 2006).

15. For example, this topic was covered in the conference held at the Miller Center of Public Affairs at the University of Virginia in June 2007. Although the conference included discussions of U.S. foreign policy in general during the next presidential administration, policy toward China specifically was a centerpiece issue. See Fareed Zakaria et al., "After the Bush Doctrine: National Security Strategy for a New Administration," Conference at the Miller Center of Public Affairs, University of Virginia, June 7, 2007. Essays from the conference will appear in Melvyn P. Leffler and Jeffrey W. Legro, eds., *To Lead the World: American Strategy after the Bush Doctrine*, (New York: Oxford University Press, 2008). In addition, see G. John Ikenberry and Robert Kagan, "The Princeton Project on National Security: International Order in a Unipolar Era," a seminar sponsored by the Carnegie Endowment for International Peace and the Woodrow Wilson School of Public and International Affairs, October 8, 2004. A summary of the seminar is available at http://www.princeton.edu/~ppns/conferences/reports/order.pdf.

16. David Brooks, "A New Global Blueprint," *New York Times*, June 19, 2007, http://select.nytimes.com/2007/06/19/opinion/19brooks.html.

17. Robert Kagan, "The Illusion of Managing China," *Washington Post*, May 15, 2005, http://www.washingtonpost.com/wp-dyn/content/article/2005/05/13/AR2005051301405.html.

18. Brooks, "New Global Blueprint."

19. "Chinese Become Sharply Negative about U.S., Americans Mildly

Negative about China," *WorldPublicOpinion.org,* April 17, 2006, http://www
.worldpublicopinion.org/incl/printable_version.php?pnt=189.

20. "Top Trading Partners—Total Trade, Exports, Imports, Foreign Trade
Statistics," U.S. Census Bureau, March 11, 2008, http://www.census.gov/foreign
-trade/statistics/highlights/toppartners.html#exports.

21. For summaries of legislation regarding China in the 108th, 109th, and
110th U.S. Congresses, see Kerry Dumbaugh, "China-U.S. Relations during the 108th Congress," Congressional Research Service, January 11, 2005,
http://www.fas.org/sgp/crs/row/RL31815.pdf; Dumbaugh, "China-U.S. Relations: Current Issues"; and Robert Sutter, "The Democratic-Led 110th Congress: Implications for Asia," *Asia Policy* 3 (January 2007), http://forbes.house
.gov/uploadedfiles/NBR.pdf.

22. "America's Fear of China," *The Economist,* May 19, 2007.

23. U.S. Department of the Treasury/Federal Reserve Board, "Major Foreign Holders of Treasury Securities," February 29, 2008, http://www.ustreas
.gov/tic/mfh.txt.

24. Sutter, "The Democratic-Led 110th Congress," 142.

25. Dumbaugh, "China-U.S. Relations: Current Issues," 27–28; Francesco
Guerrera, "CNOOC at Odds with Congress over Unocal Deal," *Financial Times,*
July 26, 2005, http://search.ft.com/ftArticle?queryText=cnooc&page=6&id
=050726007068&ct=0.

26. Sutter, "The Democratic-Led 110th Congress," 142.

27. Tom Curry, "Clinton Sounds the China Alarm as '08 Issue," *MSNBC.com,*
March 2, 2007, http://www.msnbc.msn.com/id/17403964/print/1/displaymode/
1098.

28. Ibid.

29. Scott Bittle and Jonathan Rochkind, "Loss of Faith: Public's Belief in
Effective Solutions Eroding," *Public Agenda,* Fall 2007, 20, http://www.publi-
cagenda.org/foreignpolicy/pdfs/foreign_policy_index_fall07.pdf.

30. Barack Obama, "Renewing American Leadership," *Foreign Affairs*
(July/August 2007), http://www.foreignaffairs.org/20070701faessay86401-p0/
barack-obama/renewing-american-leadership.html; Mitt Romney, "Rising to
a New Generation of Global Challenges," *Foreign Affairs* (July/August 2007),
http://www.foreignaffairs.org/20070701faessay86402/mitt-romney/rising-to
-a-new-generation-of-global-challenges.html.

31. Tom Curry, "Clinton Sounds the China Alarm as '08 Issue."

32. John McCain, "McCain Remarks—Hoover Institution," May 1, 2007,
http://media.hoover.org/documents/McCain_05-01-07.pdf.

33. U.S. Department of State, Bureau of International Information Programs, "U.S. Wants Deeper Cooperation with China, State's Zoellick Says," August 4, 2005, http://usinfo.state.gov/eap/Archive/2005/Aug/03-241723.html; "Deputy Secretary of State Zoellick to Host Second U.S.-China Senior Dialogue December 7–8, 2005," *U.S. Department of State Media Note*, December 2, 2005, http://www.state.gov/r/pa/prs/ps2005/57597.htm; "U.S. to Hold Senior Dialogue with China and Strategic Consultation for Allied Partnership Talks with Republic of Korea," *U.S. Department of State Media Note*, November 4, 2006, http://www.state.gov/r/pa/prs/ps/2006/75551.htm; "Conclusion of the Fourth U.S.-China Senior Dialogue," *U.S. Department of State Media Note*, June 21, 2007, http://www.state.gov/r/pa/prs/ps/2007/jun/86997.htm; "Fact Sheet: Creation of the U.S.-China Strategic Economic Dialogue," U.S. Department of Treasury Press Room, September 20, 2006, http://www.treas.gov/press/releases/hp107.htm; "Deputy Secretary Zoellick Statement on Conclusion of the Second U.S.-China Senior Dialogue," *U.S. Department of State Media Note*, December 8, 2005, http://www.state.gov/r/pa/ei/pix/2005ds/57825.htm.

34. Bureau of International Information Programs, "U.S. Wants Deeper Cooperation with China, State's Zoellick Says."

35. U.S. Department of Defense, *Annual Report to Congress: Military Power of the People's Republic of China, 2007* (Washington, D.C.: Office of the Secretary of Defense, 2007), 1, http://www.defenselink.mil/pubs/pdfs/070523-China-Military-Power-final.pdf.

36. Guerrera, "CNOOC at Odds"; "Giving China a Bloody Nose," *The Economist*, August 4, 2005; Ben White, "Unocal Accepts Chevron's Raised Bid," *Washington Post*, July 21, 2005, http://www.washingtonpost.com/wp-dyn/content/article/2005/07/20/AR2005072002476.html; Francesco Guerrera, Joe Leahy and Fang Wang, "Beijing 'Never Behind' Bid for Unocal," *Financial Times*, August 6, 2005, http://search.ft.com/ftArticle?queryText=unocal&page=13&id=050806000776&ct=0.

37. Guerrera, Leahy, and Wang, "Beijing 'Never Behind' Bid for Unocal."

38. "Giving China a Bloody Nose," *The Economist*, August 4, 2005.

39. See Steve A. Yetiv, and Chunlong Lu, "China, Global Energy, and the Middle East," *Middle East Journal* 61/2 (Spring 2007): 199–218; Charles E. Ziegler, "The Energy Factor in China's Foreign Policy," *Journal of Chinese Political Science* 11/1 (Spring 2006): 1–23; Jeffrey Bader and Flynt Leverett, "Managing China-U.S. Energy Competition in the Middle East," *Washington Quarterly* 29/1 (Winter 2005–2006): 187–201, http://www.twq.com/06winter/docs/06winter_leverett.pdf; David Zweig and Bi Jianhai, "China's Global Hunt for Energy," *Foreign Affairs* 84/5 (September/October 2005): 25–38; Jin Liangxiang, "Energy First: China and the Middle East," *Middle East Quarterly* (Spring

2005); Erica S. Downs, "The Chinese Energy Security Debate," *China Quarterly* 177 (March 2004): 21–41; Henry J. Kenny, "China and the Competition for Oil and Gas in Asia," *Asia-Pacific Review* 11/2 (2004): 36–47; T.S. Gopi Rethinaraj, "China's Energy and Regional Security Perspectives," *Defense & Security Analysis* 19/4 (December 2003): 377–388.

40. We are not including here a discussion of U.S. foreign aid to Middle Eastern countries, as that is not technically an economic topic. Nevertheless, aid represents a crucial pillar of the U.S.-Middle East relationship, and the United States would probably benefit strategically (if not politically) by attaching fewer—or smarter—conditions to its aid packages. Otherwise, countries that are U.S. allies will be increasingly tempted by Chinese offers having few if any conditionalities attached. See Jeremy M. Sharp, "U.S. Foreign Assistance to the Middle East: Historical Background, Recent Trends, and the FY2008 Request," Congressional Research Service, July 3, 2007, http://www.fas.org/sgp/crs/mideast/RL32260.pdf.

41. Tanya C. Hsu, "The United States Must Not Neglect Saudi Arabian Investment," *Saudi-American Forum,* September 23, 2003, http://www.saudi-american-forum.org/Newsletters/SAF_Essay_22.htm.

42. U.S. Department of Commerce, "HS Total All Merchandise: 2006 Imports from Saudi Arabia," *TradeStats Express—National Trade Data,* http://tse.export.gov/NTDChartDisplay.aspx?UniqueURL=hsjdw1n1ps3nagasetifuq55-2007-8-13-11-52-29&Flow=Import.

43. Ibrahim Nafie, "Looking East," *Al-Ahram,* May 4, 2006, http://weekly.ahram.org.eg/2006/793/op1.htm. Like the United States, China has a trade deficit with Saudi Arabia, and its imports from the Kingdom consist mostly of oil products. It is difficult to find reliable statistics suggesting whether the share of oil products as a percentage of the value of China's total imports from Saudi Arabia is higher or lower than that of the United States.

44. Energy Information Administration, "U.S. Imports by Country of Origin," May 2007, http://tonto.eia.doe.gov/dnav/pet/pet_move_impcus_a2_nus_ep00_im0_mbbl_a.htm; Ibrahim Nafie, "Looking East," *Al Ahram Weekly,* May 4–10, 2006, http://weekly.ahram.org.eg/2006/793/op1.htm.

45. EIA, "U.S. Imports by Country of Origin."

46. Erica Strecker Downs, *China's Quest for Energy Security* (Santa Monica, Calif.: RAND, 2000), 31–32.

47. See John W. Garver's table 2.1, "Chinese Investments and Energy Ties with Middle East and North African Countries," in this volume, p.25.

48. "Saudi Arabia," U.S. Trade Representative, 2005, http://www.ustr.gov/assets/Document_Library/Reports_Publications/2005/2005_NTE_Report/asset_upload_file331_7522.pdf.

49. U.S. Trade Representative, "U.S. Data for Given Trade Partners in Rank Order of US Goods Exports," 2007, http://www.ustr.gov/assets/Document_Library/Reports_Publications/2007/2007_NTE_Report/asset_upload_file670_10924.pdf?ht=.

50. Mushtak Parker, "Kingdom Strives to Become Top FDI Location," *Arab News*, October 10, 2005, http://www.arabnews.com/?page=6&section=0&article=71477&d=10&m=10&y=2005.

51. The most comprehensive account of these sales and purchases is Blumenthal, "Providing Arms." Further details on the Israel relationship can be found in P.R. Kumaraswamy, "At What Cost Israel-China Ties?" *Middle East Quarterly* (Spring 2006): 37–44. See also Jephraim Gundzik, "The Ties That Bind: China, Russia, and Iran," *Asia Times,* June 4, 2005, http://www.atimes.com/atimes/China/GF04Ad07.html; Sudha Ramachandran, "US up in Arms over Sino-Israel Ties," *Asia Times*, December 21, 2004, http://www.atimes.com/atimes/Middle_East/FL21Ak01.html; Richard L. Russell, "China's WMD Foot in the Greater Middle East's Door," *MERIA* 9/3 (September 2005), http://meria.idc.ac.il/journal/2005/issue3/jv9no3a6.html; Simon Henderson, "Chinese-Saudi Cooperation: Oil But Also Missiles," *Policy Watch #1095*, April 21, 2006, http://www.washingtoninstitute.org/templateC05.php?CID=2460.

52. Shirley A. Kan, "China and Proliferation of Weapons of Mass Destruction and Missiles: Policy Issues," Congressional Research Service, May 9, 2007, 1, http://www.fas.org/sgp/crs/nuke/RL31555.pdf.

53. Frida Berrigan, "United States Rides Weapons Bonanza Wave," *Foreign Policy in Focus,* November 16, 2006, http://www.fpif.org/fpiftxt/3715.

54. Bryan Bender, "U.S. is Top Purveyor on Weapons Sales List: Shipments Grow to Unstable Areas," *Boston Globe*, November 13, 2006, http://www.boston.com/news/world/articles/2006/11/13/us_is_top_purveyor_on_weapons_sales_list/.

55. Richard F. Grimmett, "U.S. Arms Sales: Agreements with and Deliveries to Major Clients, 1996–2003," Congressional Research Service, December 8, 2004, 9, http://www.fas.org/man/crs/RL32689.pdf.

56. Jonathan Reingold, "U.S. Arms Sales to Israel End Up in China, Iraq," *Common Dreams News Center*, May 9, 2002, http://www.commondreams.org/cgi-bin/print.cgi?file=/views02/0509-07.htm.

57. See "Unclassified Report to Congress on the Acquisition of Technology Relating to Weapons of Mass Destruction and Advanced Conventional Munitions, 1 July through 31 December 2003," *Central Intelligence Agency Reports.*

58. U.S. Department of Defense, *Quadrennial Defense Review Report 2006,* 29.

59. Tarique Niazi, "Gwadar: China's Naval Outpost on the Indian Ocean," *Jamestown Foundation China Brief*, February 16, 2005, http://www.jamestown.org/news_details.php?news_id=93.

60. BBC News, "U.S. 'Aims to Help' Mid-East Allies," July 31, 2007, http://news.bbc.co.uk/2/hi/middle_east/6924273.stm.

61. For a discussion of this, see Anthony Bubalo, "US Frictions Have United Asia and Mideast Groups," *Financial Times,* October 13, 2005, http://search.ft.com/nonFtArticle?id=051013000750.

62. Khaled al Maeena, "Guantanamo Is America's Greatest Shame," *Arab View*, June 20, 2007, http://www.arabview.com/articles.asp?article=870; Ivan Eland, "China Returns Fire on U.S. Human Rights Abuses," *The Independent Institute*, March 12, 2007, http://www.independent.org/newsroom/article.asp?id=1939.

63. "Asia: China: U.S. Sends Chinese Guantánamo Detainees to Albania," *New York Times*, May 6, 2006, http://query.nytimes.com/gst/fullpage.html?res=9407E2D91F3FF935A35756C0A9609C8B63.

64. Carol Migdalovitz, "Israeli-Arab Negotiations: Background, Conflicts, and U.S. Policy," Congressional Research Service, July 7, 2007, 1, http://www.fas.org/sgp/crs/mideast/RL33530.pdf.

65. "Palestinian FM to Visit China," *The Weekly Press Review of the Swiss Embassy in the People's Republic of China*, May 18, 2006, http://www.sinoptic.ch/embassy/presseschau/2006/20060515-0519.htm.

66. "A Quintet, Anyone?" *The Economist,* January 11, 2007.

67. Hassan Tahsin, "America's True Intentions in the Middle East," *Arab View*, December 29, 2006, http://www.arabview.com/articles.asp?article=768.

68. People's Republic of China, Ministry of Foreign Affairs, "United States of America: Bilateral Relations," April 2, 2004.

CHAPTER FIVE

CONCLUSION AND RECOMMENDATIONS

KEY FINDINGS

There is a slowly growing sense in some quarters that China is emerging as a rival of the United States in the Middle East. At the same time, some in the Middle East have sought to encourage such a rivalry in an effort to advance their own interests. This study has sought to understand each party's circumstances and interests with an eye toward future developments. Over the course of this inquiry, several things have become clear:

- **The U.S. interest in the Middle East is strategic and enduring.**

For more than a half century, that interest has centered on energy security—not so much for U.S. consumers, but for the global market consisting largely of U.S. friends and allies in Europe, East Asia, and Latin America. Securing the stable, uninterrupted flow of oil at reasonable prices has remained a high priority for the United States, and promoting the stability of friendly regimes has consistently been an important means to that end. The U.S. interests in the Middle East go beyond energy, however. The United States maintains a strategic interest in the security of Israel. In addition, the global U.S. defense posture is increasingly concerned with devising effective methods to combat terrorism and other forms of asymmetrical warfare that are often tied to combatants or grievances originating in the Middle East. Other interests also help shape interests in the region, from nonproliferation to non-oil trade and investment.

The events of September 11, 2001, gave both importance and ur-
gency to the Middle East for U.S. policymakers. The region became
a focus of both presidential and public attention in the immediate aftermath of the attacks, and that attention increased still further with
the sustained U.S. military campaign in Iraq (which the September 11
attacks helped stimulate). Although future U.S. administrations are
unlikely to pursue President George W. Bush's once-vigorous efforts
to promote democracy in the Middle East, it is hard to imagine that
such administrations will feel they have the luxury to walk away from
the region in the foreseeable future. Global reliance on oil and the U.S.
role in ensuring the availability of Middle Eastern oil seem assured for
several decades to come. Also, the increasingly networked nature of
violent extremism, combined with its deep ties to the Middle East, des-
tine the United States to maintain a focus on the region long into the
future. Should the oil boom of the early twenty-first century continue,
the increasing importance of the Middle East to global financial markets is yet another inducement for U.S. engagement, as the region will
be increasingly decisive in determining international monetary flows.

At the same time, the United States remains keenly interested in
China. Although some in the United States look with alarm at China's
growing capacity and fear a rival superpower in the making, few doubt
that China's size and impressive economic growth will continue to re-
shape the global balance of power. For many Americans, their aware-
ness of China is more economic than strategic. The flood of Chinese
goods onto global markets and the rapidly growing sophistication of
Chinese manufacturers mean that Chinese products are everywhere in
the United States, from electronics to agricultural foodstuffs. China's
economic might is not seen as purely benign, nor is it confined to traditional balance of trade issues. China, like some Gulf states, created its
own $200 billion dollar sovereign wealth fund (China Investment Cor-
poration) that has already purchased stakes in major Western firms.
Other Chinese companies have attempted to buy interests in U.S. business sectors that have national security implications including energy
and advanced electronics and communications systems. Even within
its own borders China's actions arouse anxiety among Americans—
from business practices that disadvantage foreign investors to labor
practices that help allow Chinese manufacturers to underbid many
producers around the world to environmental degradation. Concern

about Chinese human rights practices remains an issue, as do Chinese relations with authoritarian regimes around the world.

Of somewhat less public interest, but of keen governmental interest, is the military equation with China. The Pacific is a key theater for U.S. military engagement, and the United States maintains more than 300,000 military personnel focused on the region.[1] U.S. partnerships with Korea, Japan, and Australia are long-standing and robust. The recent deepening of the U.S-Indian relationship is sometimes perceived in China as adding to an alliance structure in which China is encircled by regional democratic nations brought together by the United States. Additionally, the American obligation to defend Taiwan is ever present in China's strategic thought. The United States has helped enforce a *pax americana* in the region since the end of World War II, and tightly interlocking trade and military ties suggest a keen interest in maintaining a strong U.S. presence.

To a great extent, the U.S. strategic views of the Middle East and East Asia do not meet. The United States has separate military commands responsible for each area. Ongoing operations in several theaters in the Middle East serve to focus the military's effort in the region quite closely on war fighting, rather than with robust engagement and the development of a new multilateral security order subordinated to the main effort. In addition, Middle Eastern regional governments' strong preference to rely principally on bilateral relationships with the United States rather than multilateral security arrangements makes it harder for third countries such as China to play a role.

There is little U.S. involvement in China's economic engagement with the region, as U.S. and Chinese traders are often seeking to trade in very different goods for very different markets. The United States exports relatively little of the industrial and manufactured products that are China's strength, while China cannot compete on the high-level goods and services where the United States excels. The U.S. military presence, and particularly its protection of the sea-lanes between the Middle East and China, redounds significantly to Chinese benefit at no apparent cost.

Where China and the United States do interact in the Middle East, much of that interaction is seemingly conflictual. In particular, U.S. officials complain about Chinese trade agreements with nations the United States is seeking to isolate and sanction, such as Sudan and

Iran. There is also widespread concern about China and the arms trade, involving either the Chinese sale of military equipment to U.S. foes, or China's acquisition of sensitive U.S. military technology from U.S. allies. Although the Middle East is not a key locus of U.S.-Chinese conflict, the potential for greater conflict is there.

■ **Chinese interests in the Middle East are significant and growing.**

China is acutely aware of its need to import oil to support its growing economy, and much of that oil will come from the Middle East for many decades to come. That plain fact is the consequence of two realities: first, the Middle East has the largest proven reserves of oil in the world, and second, China is far closer to the Middle East than other potential sources of oil such as West Africa or Latin America. Although many Chinese scholars perceive a strategic imperative in conservation and pursuit of alternative energy, China's immediate needs suggest a deepening of economic ties to the region. Additionally, the increasingly sophisticated behavior of China's state-owned energy conglomerates demonstrates that they are no longer simply seeking equity oil to meet China's needs. This further suggests that even if China's growing demand for oil were to slow, the future prosperity of large Chinese companies is now inexorably linked to that of the global oil market as a whole and Middle East oil in particular.

Compared with the United States, however, China's interests are relatively uncomplicated. China has walked away from its past as a supporter of liberation movements, and though it feels a need to crack down on terror groups based in the far western provinces of China, those groups do not have nearly the same centrality in Chinese strategic thinking that anti-Western terror groups have in the United States. As argued here, China desires positive relations with all parties in the Middle East, and it has largely been able to achieve its goals. The fact that China has been able to build relatively close ties with both Israel and Iran is only partly a sign that neither relationship is a strategic relationship for the People's Republic; even more so, it is a sign of the deftness of Chinese diplomacy.

What is strategic to China is its relationship with the United States. Convinced that an antagonistic relationship with the United States would degrade China's interests around the globe, the Chinese government carefully weighs actions that might compromise core U.S. interests. China clearly sees the depth of U.S. engagement in the Middle

East and is loath to challenge it. To a degree, the Chinese see themselves benefiting from American missteps in the Middle East, as the United States pours resources into wars in Iraq and Afghanistan and is increasingly resented by regional publics. China seems inclined to help the United States in modest ways, but it feels no need to provide major support for U.S. policies it sees as deeply misguided.

Interestingly, China may not share the U.S. commitment to regime stability in the area. Whereas the United States is committed to securing the stability of friendly governments as a way to ensure its interests in the region, China seems more agnostic. Either China believes that it cannot make a material difference in the stability of such governments or that U.S. efforts in that regard are sufficient to safeguard China's interests. The Chinese appear to be banking on the fact that they are a sufficiently attractive market that countries will sell it oil regardless of who is in power. Maintaining a low strategic profile, in fact, helps ensure that ideological opposition to supplying China with oil does not arise.

That some Middle East governments are intrigued by the "China Model" of development—economic liberalization without corresponding liberal political evolution—is an added benefit for China. It gives China entrée into precisely the markets that many Western governments and multinational oil companies shun, and it helps create an atmosphere of partnership quite distinct from the legacy of suspicion and exploitation that many in the Middle East ascribe to their history with the West.

■ **The Middle East's interests in the United States and China are evolving.**

As recently as a few decades ago, the Middle East looked almost exclusively westward for both its markets and its security. Westerners helped develop the region's oil production, Westerners purchased much of that oil, and Westerners helped create the state of Israel in their midst. The Soviet Union had relatively less influence. For all of its efforts in the region, the Soviet Union never transcended principally military relationships with regional governments, and in the event, those relationships were mostly with relatively poorer countries such as Egypt and Syria, or very poor ones such as South Yemen. China was even more of an afterthought. The idea of developing deep ties with China seemed farfetched not only for the region's governments, but even for the armed movements that opposed them.

To a great extent, Middle Eastern countries continue to look westward. The United States remains the most powerful and most agile fighting force in the region, and it brings potent tools to the table in governments' struggle against both international and domestic terrorism. U.S. technology in everything from weaponry to software to oil recovery is the best in the world, and U.S. organizational practice—in business, government, and the military—is a consistent force multiplier in addressing problems.

Although only a handful of countries in the Middle East seek deep relationships with China to rival the kinds of relationships many others have with the United States, there is widespread curiosity about what a deeper relationship with China might hold. In part, this curiosity is driven by dissatisfaction with a U.S. presence that Middle Easterners see as both heavy-handed and incompetent. The failure to make progress on Arab-Israeli peace issues, the Pandora's box that the United States helped open in Iraq, the resurgence of Iran, and the clumsy efforts to pressure friendly Middle Eastern governments to democratize have all dimmed the promise regional governments see in a close U.S. partnership. For energy producers, the rising rhetoric of promoting energy independence in the United States, combined with relatively flat demand growth for oil in recent years, suggests that a close U.S. relationship is insufficient to protect their interests.

At the same time, China is an attractive market with its growing oil demand. Middle Eastern investors seeking to maximize the value of their investments see the same promise in China as investors all over the world. In addition, China has expressed little of the concern that has erupted in Western markets about Arab ownership of assets, and Chinese investment can be a useful hedge against fickle Western attitudes toward foreign capital.

Important, too, is a sense among many regional countries that bilateral relations with China can supplement relations with the United States without detracting from them. Even U.S. allies who would not want to provoke a full-scale rivalry between the United States and China see such relations as enhancing their bargaining positions vis-à-vis the United States. This is even truer with U.S. foes in the region that are desperate to escape from U.S. constraints and are thus willing to provide especially attractive opportunities for Chinese investors willing to defy U.S. diktats.

The United States, China, and the Middle East are not necessarily at odds, then, but there are plenty of tensions. Interests are far from identical, and each side has an interest in preventing the other two from getting too close.

China evinces no interest in confronting the United States, and two countries that appear to have tried to draw China in to balance against the United States—Iraq under Saddam Hussein and more recently Iran—have seen the Chinese preserve some distance. Still, it is not hard to imagine a set of circumstances in which U.S. officials would see Chinese actions as threatening vital U.S. interests and act accordingly. Iran is the most immediate flashpoint in this regard, but far from the only one. The repercussions of such actions would reverberate far beyond the Middle East. Equally, neither side has any interest in unconstrained rivalry in the Middle East. Such a rivalry would draw resources and close markets to one side or another, and it would degrade each country's interest rather than enhance it.

POLICY RECOMMENDATIONS: BUILDING ON SECURITY FIRST

The challenge in all of this is to boost cooperation in areas of common interests, especially at a time when the United States is feeling strategically vulnerable, is wary of China's emerging as a potential global rival, and is fiercely protective of its role in maintaining Gulf security. China, for its part, often falls back on a conception of the United States as a global hegemon; as such, China believes that the United States seeks to hem China in rather than enhance common interests.

China could be forgiven for evincing satisfaction with the current state of affairs, in which it has access to all markets, the United States alienates many of those whom it seeks to protect, and China is able to freeload on the U.S. securing of the sea-lanes. However, such a state of affairs increases the possibility of Sino-American tension that degrades the interests of each.

The one thing that is clearly in the shared interest of the United States, China, and the regional countries is security. First and foremost, the regional and global powers all want to guarantee energy security and protect energy production and transportation facilities. They also share a keen interest in preventing the region from exporting terrorism, sensitive as they are to the ways in which asymmetrical warfare poses a bigger danger to property and lives in the Middle East than the potential invasion of one country by a neighbor.

Rather than be a source of tension, the keenly shared U.S. and Chinese interests in Gulf security mean that the region can be a locus of cooperation between the two sides, working in partnership with host governments. Such cooperation can begin with participation in ship identification protocols and cargo security initiatives, and China's participation can help assure Iran that such activities are not merely a cover for anti-Iranian activities. Cooperation could continue through support for multilateral search and rescue/consequence management operations (perhaps in concert with other Asian powers, such as Japan, that share China's dependence on Gulf oil). Such practical and cooperative activities could help underline China's commitment to Gulf stability and could also inhibit potentially troublesome actors, such as Iran's Revolutionary Guard Corps, from carrying out provocative actions against shipping. Such participation would be a departure for China, which has traditionally argued that Gulf security should be the province of those countries littoral to the Gulf. Yet China's deployment of 1,000 peacekeeping troops to Lebanon in the fall of 2006 was a sign of China's willingness to consider such untraditional peacekeeping activities, and they could begin to make a material difference in Gulf security. In addition, successful Sino-American cooperation in the Gulf would help reassure China that the United States remains willing to protect Chinese maritime commercial interests as part of the interdependent global economy interests in the event of a global security incident.

The United States and China should also investigate creating a new security framework that seeks to unite key oil-producing countries in the Middle East with their most important consumers. Such an organization (which would be more comprehensive than the Shanghai Cooperation Organization) would underline the interdependence of the two groups and help promote concrete actions that build common interests in security, broadly understood. Such an organization would take some time to establish, as its goal would be to bring together potential antagonists in the region. If successfully established, however, it would provide a multilateral forum for reducing tensions. Although the organization would not be a substitute for the overwhelming importance of U.S. bilateral ties in securing energy in the region, joint activities and understandings could play a constructive role highlighting common interests and encouraging burden sharing among beneficiaries.

There are other fronts in which cooperation is less promising. The issue of Israel reveals a clear divergence between China and the United States. China views Israel as an important ally, but it lacks the strategic commitment to protect the Jewish state that is part of the bedrock of U.S. policy toward the Middle East. Israel's closeness to the United States has contributed to U.S. influence over Israeli arms sales to China, thereby helping to curtail the Israel-China military relationship. Given the intimacy of the U.S.-Israel relationship, this is perhaps to be expected, but it suggests limits to the relationships that the United States will allow its allies to build with China.

At the same time, China's desire to remain aloof from the divisive struggles of the Middle East suggests relatively little utility to drawing China into a central role in Arab-Israeli peacemaking. Such a role requires a willingness to pressure as well as cajole, and China's inclination seems to tend much more toward cajoling, while leaving the pressuring to the United States and others. Rather than build trust between the United States, China, and the Middle Eastern states, higher-profile Chinese engagement on Arab-Israeli peacemaking seems far more likely to escalate complaints of bias and mercenary behavior. As so, it would be neither in the U.S. or Chinese interest.

On the commercial score, it is hard to see the Sino-American relationship in the Middle East as anything but a rivalry, and that rivalry seems destined to grow. Chinese economic sophistication is increasing, and the U.S. manufacturing sector continues to shrink. As Chinese entities pick up more skills, they will edge still closer to fields controlled by Western firms. There are few incentives for the Chinese to cooperate more with an economic competitor, especially as the United States hobbles itself both by pursuing unilateral sanctions against various entities and governments and by adhering to anti-bribery legislation that creates opportunities for eager, but less scrupulous, competitors. In this, Sino-American relations and China's relations with the states of the region seem utterly unremarkable. The same pattern is playing out around the world, which does not seem the cause for much alarm here or elsewhere.

There is little question that the Middle East can emerge as a key bone of contention between the United States and China, exacerbating what is already a sometimes tense relationship. The U.S. government sees the region as the most critical in the world; witness the commitment of resources it continues to make in regional stability. It would be easy for China to be seen as a spoiler in this vital region, poisoning not only cooperation in the Middle East, but also farther afield. Further, some regional countries seem to see an interest in stoking a rivalry between the United States and China as a way of advancing their own interests. They do so either by encouraging China to evade U.S.-led sanctions or encouraging a bidding war between the two sides. Whereas some in the Middle East may see such a rivalry to their advantage, such a rivalry would be likely to diminish regional security rather than enhance it, leave regional powers less secure than they already are, and certainly undermine the prospects of Sino-American cooperation in the region and farther afield.

Instead, each side—China, the United States, and the Middle East—has a deep interest in promoting greater cooperation throughout the "vital triangle," recognizing common interests and acting in such a way as to promote them in concert. Such cooperation would have the benefit not only of enhancing security in the Middle East, but also of creating a pattern of security cooperation between the United States and China that would infuse a host of other engagements around the world.

Note

1. U.S. Pacific Command, "PACOM Fact Sheet," www.pacom.mil/about/pacom.shtml.

INDEX

Page numbers followed by the letters *f* and *t* refer to figures and tables, respectively. Page numbers followed by the letter *n* refer to end-of-chapter notes.

ABOUT THE AUTHORS

Jon B. Alterman is director and senior fellow of the CSIS Middle East Program. Prior to joining CSIS, he served as a member of the Policy Planning Staff at the U.S. Department of State and as a special assistant to the assistant secretary of state for Near Eastern affairs. He served as an expert adviser to the Iraq Study Group (also known as the Baker-Hamilton Commission) and is a professorial lecturer at the Johns Hopkins School of Advanced International Studies and the George Washington University.

Before entering government, Alterman was a scholar at the U.S. Institute of Peace and at the Washington Institute for Near East Policy. From 1993 to 1997, he was an award-winning teacher at Harvard University, where he received a Ph.D. in history. He also worked as a legislative aide to Senator Daniel P. Moynihan (D-N.Y.), responsible for foreign policy and defense. Alterman has lectured in more than 25 countries on subjects related to the Middle East and U.S. policy toward the region.

He is the author or coauthor of three other books and editor of two more. In addition to his academic work, he is a frequent commentator in print, on radio, and on television. His opinion pieces have appeared in the *Washington Post, Los Angeles Times, Wall Street Journal, Financial Times, Asharq al-Awsat*, and other major publications. Alterman is a member of the editorial boards of the *Middle East Journal* and *Arab Media and Society* and is a former international affairs fellow at the Council on Foreign Relations.

John W. Garver is a professor in the Sam Nunn School of International Affairs at Georgia Tech. He is a member of the editorial boards of the journals *China Quarterly*, *Journal of Contemporary China*, *Issues and Studies*, and *Asian Security*, and is a member of the National Committee on U.S.-China Relations.

Garver is the author of seven books and more than 60 articles dealing with China relations. His books include *China and Iran: Ancient Partners in a Post-Imperial World* (2006); *Protracted Contest: Sino-Indian Rivalry in the Twentieth Century* (2001); *Face Off: China, the United States, and Taiwan's Democratization* (1997); *The Sino-American Alliance: Nationalist China and American Cold War Strategy in Asia* (1997); *The Foreign Relations of the People's Republic of China* (1993); *Chinese-Soviet Relations, 1937–1945: The Diplomacy of Chinese Nationalism* (1988); and *China's Decision for Rapprochement with the United States* (1982).

Dr. Garver has received grants from the Fulbright Foundation, the Smith Richardson Foundation, the U.S. National Academy of Science, the U.S. Department of Education, the Chiang Ching-kuo Foundation, and the U.S. Institute for Pakistan Studies. He has lived in various parts of China for more than six years, has traveled widely throughout Asia, has conducted formal research in a number of Asian countries, and is fluent in Chinese. He served in the U.S. Army from 1969 to 1971.